THE
SACRED FORMULAS
OF THE CHEROKEES
BY
JAMES MOONEY

ISBN: 9798835146864

7TH ANNUAL REPORT,

BUREAU OF AMERICAN ETHNOLOGY. PP. 302-97

ORIGINALLY PUBLISHED IN 1891

TABLE OF CONTENTS

AND THIS ALSO IS FOR TREATING THE CRIPPLER

THIS IS TO TREAT THEM IF THEY ARE BITTEN BY A SNAKE

TO TREAT THEM WHEN SOMETHING IS CAUSING SOMETHING TO EAT THEM

TO TREAT GÛⁿWANI'GISTÛ'ⁿÏ--(SECOND).

THIS TELLS ABOUT MOVING PAINS IN THE TEETH (NEURALGIA?).

TO TREAT THE GREAT CHILL

THIS IS TO MAKE CHILDREN JUMP DOWN

TO TREAT THE BLACK YELLOWNESS

TO TREAT FOR ORDEAL DISEASES

CONCERNING HUNTING

THIS IS FOR HUNTING BIRDS

TO SHOOT DWELLERS IN THE WILDERNESS

BEAR SONG

THIS IS FOR CATCHING LARGE FISH

CONCERNING LIVING HUMANITY (LOVE)

THIS TELLS ABOUT GOING INTO THE WATER

SONG FOR PAINTING

TO ATTRACT AND FIX THE AFFECTIONS

FOR SEPARATION (OF LOVERS)

TO FIX THE AFFECTIONS

TO SHORTEN A NIGHT-GOER ON THIS SIDE

I HAVE LOST SOMETHING

THIS IS TO FRIGHTEN A STORM

WHAT THOSE WHO HAVE BEEN TO WAR DID TO HELP THEMSELVES

TO DESTROY LIFE

THIS CONCERNS THE BALL PLAY--TO TAKE THEM TO WATER WITH IT

INTRODUCTION

The sacred formulas here given are selected from a collection of about six hundred, obtained on the Cherokee reservation in North Carolina in 1887 and 1888, and covering every subject pertaining to the daily life and thought of the Indian, including medicine, love, hunting, fishing, war, self-protection, destruction of enemies, witchcraft, the crops, the council, the ball play, etc., and, in fact, embodying almost the whole of the ancient religion of the Cherokees. The original manuscripts, now in the possession of. the Bureau of Ethnology, were written by the shamans of the tribe, for their own use, in the Cherokee characters invented by Sikwâ'ya (Sequoyah) in 1821, and were obtained, with the explanations, either from the writers themselves or from their surviving relatives.

Some of these manuscripts are known to be at least thirty years old, and many are probably older. The medical formulas of all kinds constitute perhaps one-half of the whole number, while the love charms come next in number, closely followed by the songs and prayers used in hunting and fishing. The great number of love charms will doubtless be a surprise to those who have been educated in the old theory that, the Indian is insensible to the attractions of woman. The comparatively small number of war formulas is explained by the fact that the last war in which the Cherokees, as a tribe, were engaged on their own account, closed with the Revolutionary period, so that these things were well nigh forgotten before the invention of the alphabet, a generation later. The Cherokees who engaged in the Creek war and the late American civil war fought in the interests of the whites, and their leaders were subordinated to white officers, hence there was not the same opportunity for the exercise of shamanistic rites that there would have been had Indians alone been concerned. The prayers for hunting, fishing, and the ball play being in more constant demand, have been better preserved,

These, formulas had been handed down orally from a remote antiquity until the early part of the present century, when the invention of the Cherokee syllabary enabled the priests of the tribe to put them into writing. The same invention made it possible for their rivals, the missionaries, to give to the Indians the Bible in their own language, so that the opposing forces of Christianity and shamanism alike profited by the genius of Sikwâya. The pressure of the new civilization was too strong to be withstood, however, and though the prophets of the old religion still have much influence with the people, they are daily losing ground and will soon be without honor in their own country.

Such an exposition of the aboriginal religion could be obtained from no other tribe in North America, for the simple reason that no other tribe has an alphabet of its own in which to record its sacred lore. It is true that the Crees and Micmacs of Canada and the Tukuth of Alaska have so-called alphabets or ideographic systems invented for their use by the missionaries, while, before the Spanish conquest, the Mayas of Central America were accustomed to note down their hero legends and priestly ceremonials in hieroglyphs graven upon the walls of their temples or painted upon tablets made of the leaves of the maguey. But it seems never to have occurred to the northern tribes that an alphabet coming from a missionary source could be used for any other purpose than the transcription of bibles and catechisms, while the sacred books of the Mayas, with a few exceptions, have long since met destruction at the hands of fanaticism, and the modern copies which have come down to the present day are written out from imperfect memory by Indians who had been educated under Spanish influences in the language, alphabet and ideas of the conquerors, and who, as is proved by an examination of the contents of the books themselves, drew from European sources a great part of their material. Moreover, the Maya tablets were so far hieratic as to be understood, only by the priests and those who had received a special training in this direction, and they seem therefore to have been entirely unintelligible to the common people.

The Cherokee alphabet, on the contrary, is the invention or adaptation of one of the tribe, who, although he borrowed most of the Roman letters, in addition to the forty or more characters of his own devising, knew nothing of their proper use or value, but reversed them or altered their forms to suit his purpose, and gave them a name and value determined by himself. This alphabet was at once adopted by the tribe for all purposes for which writing can be used, including the recording of their shamanistic prayers and ritualistic ceremonies. The formulas here given, as well as those of the entire collection, were written out by the shamans themselves--men who adhere to the ancient religion and speak only their native language in order that their sacred knowledge might be preserved in a systematic manner for their mutual benefit. The language, the conception, and the execution are all genuinely Indian, and hardly a dozen lines of the hundreds of formulas show a trace of the influence of the white man or his religion. The formulas contained in these manuscripts are not disjointed fragments of a system long since extinct, but are the revelation of a living faith which still has its priests and devoted adherents, and it is only necessary to witness a ceremonial ball play, with its fasting, its going to water, and its mystic bead manipulation, to understand how strong is the hold which the old faith yet has upon the minds even of the younger generation. The numerous archaic and figurative expressions used require the interpretation of the priests, but, as before stated, the alphabet in which they are written is that in daily use among the common people.

In all tribes that still retain something of their ancient organization we find this sacred knowledge committed to the keeping of various secret societies, each of which has its peculiar ritual with regular initiation and degrees of advancement. From this analogy we may reasonably conclude that such was formerly the case with the Cherokees also, but by the breaking down of old customs consequent upon their long contact with the whites and the voluntary adoption of a civilized form of government in 1827, all traces of such society organization have long since disappeared, and at present each priest or shaman is isolated and independent, sometimes confining himself to a particular specialty, such as love or medicine, or even the treatment of two or three diseases, in other cases broadening his field of operations to include the whole range of mystic knowledge.

It frequently happens, however, that priests form personal friendships and thus are led to divulge their secrets to each other for their mutual advantage. Thus when one shaman meets another who he thinks can probably give him some valuable information, he says to him, "Let us sit down together." This is understood by the other to mean, "Let us tell each other our secrets." Should it seem probable that the seeker after knowledge can give as much as he receives, an agreement is generally arrived at, the two retire to some convenient spot secure from observation, and the first party begins by reciting one of his formulas with the explanations. The other then reciprocates with one of his own, unless it appears that the bargain is apt to prove a losing one, in which case the conference comes to an abrupt ending.

It is sometimes possible to obtain a formula by the payment of a coat, a quantity of cloth, or a sum of money. Like the Celtic Druids of old, the candidate for the priesthood in former times found it necessary to cultivate a long memory, as no formula was repeated more than once for his benefit. It was considered that one who failed to remember after the first hearing was not worthy to be accounted a shaman. This task, however, was not so difficult as might appear on first thought, when once the learner understood the theory involved, as the formulas are all constructed on regular principles, with constant repetition of the same set of words. The obvious effect of such a regulation was to increase the respect in which this sacred knowledge was held by restricting it to the possession of a chosen few.

Although the written formulas can be read without difficulty by any Cherokee educated in his own language, the shamans take good care that their sacred writings shall not fall into the hands of the laity or of their rivals in occult practices, and in performing the ceremonies the words used are uttered in such a low tone of voice as to be unintelligible even to the one for whose benefit the formula is repeated. Such being the case, it is in order to explain how the formulas collected were obtained.

HOW THE FORMULAS WERE OBTAINED

On first visiting the reservation in the summer of 1887, I devoted considerable time to collecting plants used by the Cherokees for food or medicinal purposes, learning at the same time their Indian names and the particular uses to which each was applied and the mode of preparation. It soon became evident that the application of the medicine was not the whole, and in fact was rather the subordinate, part of the treatment, which was always accompanied by certain ceremonies and "words." From the workers employed at the time no definite idea could be obtained as to the character of these words. One young woman, indeed, who had some knowledge of the subject, volunteered to write the words which she used in her prescriptions, but failed to do so, owing chiefly to the opposition of the half-breed shamans, from whom she had obtained her information.

THE SWIMMER MANUSCRIPT

Some time afterward an acquaintance was formed with a man named A`yûⁿ'inï or "Swimmer," who proved to be so intelligent that I spent several days with him, procuring information in regard to myths and old customs. He told a number of stories in very good style, and finally related the Origin of the Bear[1]. The bears were formerly a part of the Cherokee tribe who decided to leave their kindred and go into the forest. Their friends followed them and endeavored to induce them to return, but the Ani-Tsâ'kahï, as they were called, were determined to go. Just before parting from their relatives at the edge of the forest, they turned to them and said, "It is better for you that we should go; but we will teach you songs, and some day when you are in want of food come out to the woods and sing these songs and we shall appear and give you meat." Their friends, after warning several songs from them, started back to their homes, and after proceeding a short distance, turned around to take one last look, but saw only a number of bears disappearing in the depths of the forest. The songs which they learned are still sung by the hunter to attract the bears.

When Swimmer had finished the story he was asked if he knew these songs. He replied that he did, but on being requested to sing one he made some excuse and was silent. After some further efforts the interpreter said it would be useless to press the matter then as there were several other Indians present, but that to-morrow we should have him alone with us and could then make another attempt.

The next day Swimmer was told that if he persisted in his refusal it would be necessary to employ some one else, as it was unfair in him to furnish incomplete information when he was paid to tell all he knew. He replied that he was willing to tell anything in regard to stories and customs, but that these songs were a part of his secret knowledge and commanded a high price from the hunters, who sometimes paid as much as $5 for a single song, "because you can't kill any bears or deer unless you sing them."

He was told that the only object in asking about the songs was to put them on record and preserve them, so that when he and the half dozen old men of the tribe were dead the world might be aware how much the Cherokees had known. This appeal to his professional pride

[1] To appear later with the collection of Cherokee myths

proved effectual, and when he was told that a great many similar songs had been sent to Washington by medicine men of other tribes, he promptly declared that he knew as much as any of them, and that he would give all the information in his possession, so that others might be able to judge for themselves who knew most. The only conditions he made were that these secret matters should be heard by no one else but the interpreter, and should not be discussed when other Indians were present.

As soon as the other shamans learned what was going on they endeavored by various means to persuade him to stop talking, or failing in this, to damage his reputation by throwing out hints as to his honesty or accuracy of statement. Among other objections which they advanced was one which, however incomprehensible to a white man, was perfectly intelligible to an Indian, viz.: That when he had told everything this information would be taken to Washington and locked up there, and thus they would be deprived of the knowledge. This objection was one of the most difficult to overcome, as there was no line of argument with which to oppose it.

These reports worried Swimmer, who was extremely, sensitive in regard to his reputation, and he became restive under the insinuations of his rivals. Finally on coming to work one day he produced a book from under his ragged coat as he entered the house, and said proudly: "Look at that and now see if I don't know something." It was a small day-book of about 240 pages, procured originally from a white man, and was about half filled with writing in the Cherokee characters. A brief examination disclosed the fact that it contained just those matters that had proved so difficult to procure. Here were prayers, songs, and prescriptions for the cure of all kinds of diseases--for chills, rheumatism, frostbites, wounds, bad dreams, and witchery; love charms, to gain the affections of a woman or to cause her to hate a detested rival; fishing charms, hunting charms--including the songs without which none could ever hope to kill, any game; prayers to make the corn grow, to frighten away storms, and to drive off witches; prayers for long life, for safety among strangers, for acquiring influence in council and success in the ball play. There were prayers to the Long Man, the Ancient White, the Great Whirlwind, the Yellow Rattlesnake, and to a hundred other gods of the Cherokee pantheon. It was in fact an Indian ritual and pharmacopoeia.

After recovering in a measure from the astonishment produced by this discovery I inquired whether other shamans had such books. "Yes," said Swimmer, "we all have them." Here then was a clew to follow up. A bargain was made by which be was to have another blank book into which to copy the formulas, after which the original was bought. It is now deposited in the library of the Bureau of Ethnology. The remainder of the time until the return was occupied in getting an understanding of the contents of the book.

THE GATIGWANASTI MANUSCRIPT

Further inquiry elicited the names of several others who might be supposed to have such papers. Before leaving a visit was paid to one of these, a young man named Wilnoti, whose father, Gatigwanasti, had been during his lifetime a prominent shaman, regarded as a man of superior intelligence. Wilnoti, who is a professing Christian, said that his father had had such papers, and after some explanation from the chief he consented to show them. He produced a box containing a lot of miscellaneous papers, testaments, and hymn-books, all in the Cherokee alphabet. Among them was his father's chief treasure, a manuscript book containing 122 pages of foolscap size, completely filled with formulas of the same kind as those contained in Swimmer's book. There were also a large number of loose sheets, making in all nearly 200 foolscap pages of sacred formulas.

On offering to buy the papers, he replied that he wanted to keep them in order to learn and practice these things himself--thus showing how thin was the veneer of Christianity, in his case at least. On representing to him that in a few years the new conditions would render such knowledge valueless with the younger generation, and that even if he retained the papers he would need some one else to explain them to him, he again refused, saying that they might fall into the hands of Swimmer, who, he was determined, should never see his father's papers. Thus the negotiations came to an end for the time.

On returning to the reservation in July, 1888, another effort was made to get possession of the Gatigwanasti manuscripts and any others of the same kind which could be procured. By this time the Indians had had several months to talk over the matter, and the idea had gradually dawned upon them that instead of taking their knowledge away from them and looking it up in a box, the intention was to preserve it to the world and pay them for it at the same time. In addition the writer took every opportunity to impress upon them the fact that he was acquainted with the secret knowledge of other tribes and perhaps could give them as much as they gave. It was now much easier to approach them, and on again visiting Wilnoti, in company with the interpreter, who explained the matter fully to him, he finally consented to lend the papers for a time, with the same condition that neither Swimmer nor anyone else but the chief and interpreter should see them, but he still refused to sell them. However, this allowed the use of the papers, and after repeated efforts during a period of several weeks, the matter ended in the purchase of the papers outright, with unreserved permission to show them for copying or explanation to anybody who might be selected. Wilnoti was not of a mercenary disposition, and after the first negotiations the chief difficulty was to overcome his objection to parting with his father's handwriting, but it was an essential point to get the originals, and he was allowed to copy some of the more important formulas, as he found it utterly out of the question to copy the whole.

These papers of Gatigwanasti are the most valuable of the whole, and amount to fully one-half the entire collection, about fifty pages consisting of love charms. The formulas are beautifully written in bold Cherokee characters, and the directions and headings are generally explicit, bearing out the universal testimony that he was a man of unusual intelligence and ability, characteristics inherited by his son, who, although a young man and speaking no English, is one of the most progressive and thoroughly reliable men of the band.

THE GAHUNI MANUSCRIPT

The next book procured was obtained from a woman named Ayâsta, "The Spoiler," and had been written by her husband, Gahuni, who died about 30 years ago. The matter was not difficult to arrange, as she had already been employed on several occasions, so that she understood the purpose of the work, besides which her son had been regularly engaged to copy and classify the manuscripts already procured. The book was claimed as common property by Ayâsta and her three sons, and negotiations had to be carried on with each one, although in this instance the cash amount involved was only half a dollar, in addition to another book into which to copy some family records and personal memoranda. The book contains only eight formulas, but these are of a character altogether unique, the directions especially throwing a curious light on Indian beliefs. There had been several other formulas of the class called Y'û'nnwëhï, to cause hatred between man and wife, but these had been torn out and destroyed by Ayâsta on the advice of an old shaman, in order that her sons might never learn them. In referring to the matter she spoke in a whisper, and it was evident enough that she had full faith in the deadly power of these spells.

In addition to the formulas the book contains about twenty pages of Scripture extracts in the same handwriting, for Gahuni, like several others of their shamans, combined the professions of Indian conjurer and Methodist preacher. After his death the book fell into the hands of the younger members of the family, who filled it with miscellaneous writings and scribblings. Among other things there are about seventy pages of what was intended to be a Cherokee-English pronouncing dictionary, probably written by the youngest son, already mentioned, who has attended school, and who served for some time as copyist on the formulas. This curious Indian production, of which only a few columns are filled out, consists of a list of simple English words and phrases, written in ordinary English script, followed by Cherokee characters intended to give the approximate pronunciation, together with the corresponding word in the Cherokee language and characters. As the language lacks a number of sounds which are of frequent occurrence in English, the attempts to indicate the pronunciation sometimes give amusing results. Thus we find: Fox (English script); *kwâgisï'* (Cherokee characters); *tsú`lû'* (Cherokee characters). As the Cherokee language lacks the labial *f* and has no compound sound equivalent to our *x,kwâgisï'* is as near as the

Cherokee speaker can come to pronouncing our word fox. In the same way "bet" becomes *wëtï*, and "sheep" is *síkwï*, while "if he has no dog" appears in the disguise of *ikwï hâsï nâ dâ'ga*.

THE INÂLI MANUSCRIPT

In the course of further inquiries in regard to the whereabouts of other manuscripts of this kind we heard a great deal about Inâ'lï, or "Black Fox," who had died a few years before at an advanced age, and who was universally admitted to have been one of their most able men and the most prominent literary character among them, for from what has been said it must be sufficiently evident that the Cherokees have their native literature and literary men. Like those already mentioned, he was a full-blood Cherokee, speaking no English, and in the course of a long lifetime he had filled almost every position of honor among his people, including those of councilor, keeper of the townhouse records, Sunday-school leader, conjurer, officer in the Confederate service, and Methodist preacher, at last dying, as he was born, in the ancient faith of his forefathers.

On inquiring of his daughter she stated that her father had left a great many papers, most of which were still in her possession, and on receiving from the interpreter an explanation of our purpose she readily gave permission to examine and make selections from them on condition that the matter should be kept secret from outsiders. A day was appointed for visiting her, and on arriving we found her living in a comfortable log house, built by Inâ'lï himself, with her children and an ancient female relative, a decrepit old woman, with snow-white hair and vacant countenance. This was the oldest woman of the tribe, and though now so feeble and childish, she had been a veritable savage in her young days, having carried a scalp in the scalp dance in the Creek war 75 years before.

Having placed chairs for us in the shade Inâ'lï's daughter brought out a small box filled with papers of various kinds, both Cherokee and English. The work of examining these was a tedious business, as each paper had to be opened out and enough of it read to get the general drift of the contents, after which the several classes were arranged in separate piles. While in the midst of this work she brought out another box nearly as large as a small trunk, and on setting it down there was revealed to the astonished gaze such a mass of material as it had not seemed possible could exist in the entire tribe.

In addition to papers of the sort already mentioned there were a number of letters in English from various officials and religious organizations, and addressed to "Enola," to "Rev. Black Fox," and to "Black Fox, Esq," with a large number of war letters written to him by Cherokees who had enlisted in the Confederate service. These latter are all written in the Cherokee characters, in the usual gossipy style common among friends, and several of them contain important historic material in regard to the movements of the two armies in East Tennessee. Among other things was found his certificate as a Methodist preacher, dated in 1848. "Know all men by these presents that Black Fox (Cherokee) is hereby authorized to exercise his Gifts and Graces as a local preacher in M. E. Church South. "

There was found a manuscript book in Inâ'lï's handwriting containing the records of the old council of Wolftown, of which he had been secretary for several years down to the beginning of the war. This also contains some valuable materials.

There were also a number of miscellaneous books, papers, and pictures, together with various trinkets and a number of conjuring stones.

In fact the box was a regular curiosity shop, and it was with a feeling akin to despair that we viewed the piles of manuscript which had to be waded through and classified.

There was a day's hard work ahead, and it was already past noon; but the woman was not done yet, and after rummaging about inside the house for a while longer she appeared with another armful of papers, which she emptied on top of the others.

This was the last straw; and finding it impossible to examine in detail such a mass of material we contented ourselves with picking out the sacred formulas and the two manuscript books containing the townhouse records and scriptural quotations and departed.

The daughter of Black Fox agreed to fetch down the other papers in a few days for further examination at our leisure; and she kept her promise, bringing with her at the same time a number of additional formulas which she had not been able to obtain before.

A large number of letters and other papers were selected from the miscellaneous lot, and these, with the others obtained from her, are now deposited also with the Bureau of Ethnology. Among other things found at this house were several beads of the old shell wampum, of whose use the Cherokees have now lost even the recollection. She knew only that they were very old and different from the common beads, but she prized them as talismans, and firmly refused to part with them.

OTHER MANUSCRIPTS

Subsequently a few formulas were obtained from an old shaman named Tsiskwa or "Bird," but they were so carelessly written as to be almost worthless, and the old mail who wrote them, being then on his dying bed, was unable to give much help in the matter. However, as he was anxious to tell what he knew all attempt was made to take down some formulas from his dictation. A few more were obtained in this way but the results were not satisfactory and the experiment was abandoned. About the same time A`wani'ta or "Young Deer," one of their best herb doctors, was engaged to collect the various plants used in medicine and describe their uses. While thus employed he wrote in a book furnished him for the purpose a number of formulas used by him in his practice, giving at the same time a verbal explanation of the theory and ceremonies. Among these was one for protection in battle, which had been used by himself and a number of other Cherokees in the late war. Another doctor named Takwati'hï or "Catawba Killer," was afterward employed on the same work and furnished some additional formulas which he had had his son write down from his dictation, he himself being unable to write. His knowledge was limited to the practice of a few specialties, but in regard to these his information was detailed and accurate. There was one for bleeding with the cupping horn. All these formulas obtained from Tsiskwa, A`wanita, and Takwtihi are now in possession of the Bureau.

THE KANÂHETA ANI-TSALAGI ETI

Among the papers thus obtained was a large number which for various reasons it was found difficult to handle or file for preservation. Many of them had been written so long ago that the ink had almost faded from the paper; others were written with lead pencil, so that in handling them the characters soon became blurred and almost illegible; a great many were written on scraps of paper of all shapes and sizes; and others again were full of omissions and doublets, due to the carelessness of the writer, while many consisted simply of the prayer, with nothing in the nature of a heading or prescription to show its purpose.

Under the circumstances it was deemed expedient to have a number of these formulas copied in more enduring form. For this purpose it was decided to engage the services of Ayâsta's youngest son, an intelligent young man about nineteen years of age, who had attended school long enough to obtain a fair acquaintance with English in addition to his intimate knowledge of Cherokee. He was also gifted with a ready comprehension, and from his mother and uncle Tsiskwa had acquired some familiarity with many of the archaic expressions used in the sacred formulas. He was commonly known as "Will West," but signed himself W. W. Long, Long being the translation of his father's name, Gûnahi'ta. After being instructed as to how the work should be done with reference to paragraphing, heading, etc., he was furnished a blank book of two hundred pages into which to copy such formulas as it seemed desirable to duplicate. He readily grasped the idea and in the course of about a month, working always under the writer's personal supervision, succeeded in completely filling the book according to the plan outlined. In addition to the duplicate formulas he wrote down a number of dance and drinking songs, obtained originally from A`yûn'inï, with about thirty miscellaneous formulas obtained from various sources. The book thus prepared is modeled on the plan of an ordinary book, with headings, table of contents, and even with an illuminated title page devised by the aid of the interpreter according to the regular Cherokee idiomatic form, and is altogether a unique specimen of Indian literary art. It contains in all two hundred and fifty-eight formulas and songs, which of course are native aboriginal productions, although the mechanical arrangement was performed under the direction of a white man. This book also, under its Cherokee title, *Kanâhe'ta Ani-Tsa'lagï E'tï* or "Ancient Cherokee Formulas," is now in the library of the Bureau.

There is still a considerable quantity of such manuscript in the hands of one or two shamans with whom there was no chance for negotiating, but an effort will be made to obtain possession of these on some future visit, should opportunity present. Those now in the Bureau library comprised by far the greater portion of the whole quantity held by the Indians, and as only a small portion of this was copied by the owners it can not be duplicated by any future collector.

CHARACTER OF THE FORMULAS--THE CHEROKEE RELIGION

It is impossible to overestimate the ethnologic importance of the materials thus obtained. They are invaluable as the genuine production of the Indian mind, setting forth in the clearest light the state of the aboriginal religion before its contamination by contact with the whites. To the psychologist and the student of myths they are equally precious. In regard to their linguistic value we may quote the language of Brinton, speaking of the sacred books of the Mayas, already referred to:

Another value they have, * * * and it is one which will be properly appreciated by any student of languages. They are, by common consent of all competent authorities, the genuine productions of native minds, cast in the idiomatic forms of the native tongue by those born to its use. No matter how fluent a foreigner becomes in a language not his own, he can never use it as does one who has been familiar with it from childhood. This general maxim is tenfold true when we apply it to a European learning an American language. The flow of thought, as exhibited in these two linguistic families, is in such different directions that no amount of practice can render one equally accurate in both. Hence the importance of studying a tongue as it is employed by natives; and hence the very high estimate I place on these "Books of Chilan Balam" as linguistic material--an estimate much increased by the great rarity of independent compositions in their own tongues by members of the native races of this continent.[1]

The same author, in speaking of the internal evidences of authenticity contained in the Popol Vuh, the sacred book of the Kichés, uses the following words, which apply equally well to these Cherokee formulas:

To one familiar with native American myths, this one bears undeniable marks of its aboriginal origin. Its frequent puerilities and inanities, its generally low and coarse range of thought and expression, its occasional loftiness of both, its strange metaphors and the prominence

[1] Brinton, D. G.: The books of Chilan Balam 10, Philadelphia, n. d., (1882

of strictly heathen names and potencies, bring it into unmistakable relationship to the true native myth.[2]

These formulas furnish a complete refutation of the assertion so frequently made by ignorant and prejudiced writers that the Indian had no religion excepting what they are pleased to call the meaning less mummeries of the medicine man. This is the very reverse of the truth. The Indian is essentially religious and contemplative, and it might almost be said that every act of his life is regulated and determined by his religious belief. It matters not that some may call this superstition. The difference is only relative. The religion of to-day has developed from the cruder superstitions of yesterday, and Christianity itself is but an outgrowth and enlargement of the beliefs and ceremonies which have been preserved by the Indian in their more ancient form. When we are willing to admit that the Indian has a religion which he holds sacred, even though it be different from our own, we can then admire the consistency of the theory, the particularity of the ceremonial and the beauty of the expression. So far from being a jumble of crudities, there is a wonderful completeness about the whole system which is not surpassed even by the ceremonial religions of the East. It is evident from a study of these formulas that the Cherokee Indian was a polytheist and that the spirit world was to him only a shadowy counterpart of this. All his prayers were for temporal and tangible blessings--for health, for long life, for success in the chase, in fishing, in war and in love, for good crops, for protection and for revenge. He had no Great Spirit, no happy hunting ground, no heaven, no hell, and consequently death had for him no terrors and he awaited the inevitable end with no anxiety as to the future. He was careful not to violate the rights of his tribesman or to do injury to his feelings, but there is nothing to show that he had any idea whatever of what is called morality in the abstract.

[2] Brinton, D. G: Names of the Gods in the Kiche Myths, in Proc. Am. Philos. Soc., Philadelphia, 1881, vol. 19, p. 613

THE ORIGIN OF DISEASE AND MEDICINE

In the old days quadrupeds, birds, fishes, and insects could all talk, and they and the human race lived together in peace and friendship. But as time went on the people increased so rapidly that their settlements spread over the whole earth and the poor animals found themselves beginning to be cramped for room. This was bad enough, but to add to their misfortunes man invented bows, knives, blowguns, spears, and hooks, and began to slaughter the larger animals, birds and fishes for the sake of their flesh or their skins, while the smaller creatures, such as the frogs and worms, were crushed and trodden upon without mercy, out of pure carelessness or contempt. In. this state of affairs the animals resolved to consult upon measures for their common safety.

The bears were the first to meet in council in their townhouse in Kuwa'hï, the "Mulberry Place,"[1] and the old White Bear chief presided.

After each in turn had made complaint against the way in which man killed their friends, devoured their flesh and used their skins for his own adornment, it was unanimously decided to begin war at once against the human race. Some one asked what weapons man used to accomplish their destruction. "Bows and arrows, of course," cried all the bears in chorus. "And what are they made of?" was the next question. "The bow of wood and the string of our own entrails," replied one of the bears. It was then proposed that they make a bow and some arrows and see if they could not turn man's weapons against himself. So one bear got a nice piece of locust wood and another sacrificed himself for the good of the rest in order to furnish a piece of his entrails for the string. But when everything was ready and the first bear stepped up to make the trial it was found that in letting the arrow fly after drawing back the bow, his long claws caught the string and spoiled the shot. This was annoying, but another suggested that he could overcome the difficulty by cutting his claws, which was accordingly done, and on a second trial it was found that the arrow went straight to the mark. But here the chief, the old White Bear, interposed and said that it was necessary that they should have long claws in order to be able to climb trees. "One of us has already died to furnish the bowstring, and if we now cut off our claws we shall all have to starve together. It is better to trust to the teeth and claws which

---

[1] One of the high peaks of the Smoky Mountains, on the Tennessee line, near Clingman's Dome

nature has given us, for it is evident that man's weapons were not intended for us."

No one could suggest any better plan, so the old chief dismissed the council and the bears dispersed to their forest haunts without having concerted any means for preventing the increase of the human race. Had the result of the council been otherwise, we should now be at war with the bears, but as it is the hunter does not even ask the bear's pardon when he kills one.

The deer next held a council under their chief, the Little Deer, and after some deliberation resolved to inflict rheumatism upon every hunter who should kill one of their number, unless he took care to ask their pardon for the offense. They sent notice of their decision to the nearest settlement of Indians and told them at the same time how to make propitiation when necessity forced them to kill one of the deer tribe. Now, whenever the hunter brings down a deer, the Little Deer, who is swift as the wind and can not be wounded, runs quickly up to the spot and bending over the blood stains asks the spirit of the deer if it has heard the prayer of the hunter for pardon. If the reply be "Yes" all is well and the Little Deer goes on his way, but if the reply be in the negative he follows on the trail of the hunter, guided by the drops of blood on the ground, until he arrives at the cabin in the settlement, when the Little Deer enters invisibly and strikes the neglectful hunter with rheumatism, so that he, is rendered on the instant a helpless cripple. No hunter who has regard for his health ever fails to ask pardon of the deer for killing it, although some who have not learned the proper formula may attempt to turn aside the Little Deer from his pursuit by building a fire behind them in the trail.

Next came the fishes and reptiles, who had their own grievances against humanity. They held a joint council and determined to make their victims dream of snakes twining about them in slimy folds and blowing their fetid breath in their faces, or to make them dream of eating raw or decaying fish, so that they would lose appetite, sicken, and die. Thus it is that snake and fish dreams are accounted for.

Finally the birds, insects, and smaller animals came together for a like purpose, and the Grubworm presided over the deliberations. It was decided that each in turn should express an opinion and then vote on the question as to whether or not man should be deemed guilty. Seven votes were to be sufficient to condemn him. One after another denounced man's cruelty and injustice toward the other animals and voted in favor of his death. The Frog (walâ'sï) spoke first and said: "We must do something to check the increase of the race or people will become so numerous that we shall be crowded from off the earth. See how man has kicked me about because I'm ugly, as he says, until my back is covered with sores;" and here he showed the spots on his skin. Next came the Bird (tsi'skwa; no particular species is indicated), who condemned man because "he burns my feet off," alluding to the way in which the hunter barbecues birds by impaling them on a stick set over the fire, so that their feathers and tender feet are singed and burned. Others followed in the same strain. The Ground Squirrel alone ventured to say a word in behalf of man, who seldom hurt him because he was so small; but this so enraged the others that they fell upon the Ground Squirrel and tore him with their teeth and claws, and the stripes remain on his back to this day.

The assembly then began to devise and name various diseases, one after another, and had not their invention finally failed them not one of the human race would have been able to survive. The Grubworm in his place of honor hailed each new malady with delight, until at last they had reached the end of the list, when some one suggested that it be arranged so that menstruation should sometimes prove fatal to woman. On this he rose up in his place and cried: "Wata'^{n}! Thanks! I'm glad some of them will die, for they are getting so thick that they tread on me." He fairly shook with joy at the thought, so that he fell over backward and could not get on his feet again, but had to wriggle off on his back, as the Grubworm has done ever since.

When the plants, who were friendly to man, heard what had been done by the animals, they determined to defeat their evil designs. Each tree, shrub, and herb, down even to the grasses and mosses, agreed to furnish a remedy for some one of the diseases named, and each said: "I shall appear to help man when he calls upon me in his need." Thus did medicine originate, and the plants, every one of which has its use if we only knew it, furnish the antidote to counteract the evil wrought by the revengeful animals. When the doctor is in doubt what treatment to apply for the relief of a patient, the spirit of the plant suggests to him the proper remedy.

THEORY OF DISEASE--ANIMALS, GHOSTS, WITCHES

Such is the belief upon which their medical practice is based, and whatever we may think of the theory it must be admitted that the practice is consistent in all its details with the views set forth in the myth. Like most primitive people the Cherokees believe that disease and death are not natural, but are due to the evil influence of animal spirits, ghosts, or witches. Haywood, writing in 1823, states on the authority of two intelligent residents of the Cherokee nation:

In ancient times the Cherokees had no conception of anyone dying a natural death. They universally ascribed the death of those who perished by disease to the intervention or agency of evil spirits and witches and conjurers who had connection with the Shina (Anisgi'na) or evil spirits. * * * A person dying by disease and charging his death to have been procured by means of witchcraft or spirits, by any other person, consigns that person to inevitable death. They profess to believe that their conjurations have no effect upon white men.[1]

On the authority of one of the same informants, he also mentions the veneration which "their physicians have for the numbers four and seven, who say that after man was placed upon the earth four and seven nights were instituted for the cure of diseases in the human body and the seventh night as the limit for female impurity."[2]

Viewed from a scientific standpoint, their theory and diagnosis are entirely wrong, and consequently we can hardly expect their therapeutic system to be correct. As the learned Doctor Berendt states, after an exhaustive study of the medical books of the Mayas, the scientific value of their remedies is "next to nothing." It must be admitted that many of the plants used in their medical practice possess real curative properties, but it is equally true that many others held in as high estimation are inert. It seems probable that in the beginning the various herbs and other plants were regarded as so many fetiches and were selected from some fancied connection with the disease animal, according to the idea known to modern folklorists as the doctrine of signatures. Thus at the present day the doctor puts

[1] Haywood, John: Natural and Aboriginal History of East Tennessee, 267-8, Nashville, 1823
[2] Ibid., p. 281

into the decoction intended as a vermifuge some of the red fleshy stalks of the common purslane or chickweed (Portulaca oleracea), because these stalks somewhat resemble worms and consequently must have some occult influence over worms. Here the chickweed is a fetich precisely as is the flint arrow bead which is put into the same decoction, in order that in the same mysterious manner its sharp cutting qualities may be communicated to the liquid and enable it to cut the worms into pieces. In like manner, biliousness is called by the Cherokees dalâ'nï or "yellow," because the most apparent symptom of the disease is the vomiting by the patient of the yellow bile, and hence the doctor selects for the decoction four different herbs, each of which is also called dalânï, because of the color of the root, stalk, or flower. The same idea is carried out in the tabu which generally accompanies the treatment. Thus a scrofulous patient must abstain from eating the meat of a turkey, because the fleshy dewlap which depends from its throat somewhat resembles an inflamed scrofulous eruption. On killing a deer the hunter always makes an incision in the hind quarter and removes the hamstring, because this tendon, when severed, draws up into the flesh; ergo, any one who should unfortunately partake of the hamstring would find his limbs draw up in the same manner.

There can be no doubt that in course of time a haphazard use of plants would naturally lead to the discovery that certain herbs are efficacious in certain combinations of symptoms. These plants would thus come into more frequent use and finally would obtain general recognition in the Indian materia medica. By such a process of evolution an empiric system of medicine has grown up among the Cherokees, by which they are able to, treat some classes of ailments with some degree of success, although without any intelligent idea of the process involved. It must be remembered that our own medical system has its remote origin in the same mythic conception of disease, and that within two hundred years judicial courts have condemned women to be burned to death for producing sickness by spells and incantations, while even at the present day our faith-cure professors reap their richest harvest among people commonly supposed to belong to the intelligent classes. In the treatment of wounds the Cherokee doctors exhibit a considerable degree of skill, but as far as any internal ailment is concerned the average farmer's wife is worth all the doctors in the whole tribe.

The faith of the patient has much to do with his recovery, for the Indian has the same implicit confidence in the shaman that a child has in a more intelligent physician. The ceremonies and prayers are well calculated to inspire this feeling, and the effect thus produced upon the mind of the sick man undoubtedly reacts favorably upon his physical organization.

The following list of twenty plants used in Cherokee practice will give a better idea of the extent of their medical knowledge than could be conveyed by a lengthy dissertation. The names are given in the order in which they occur in the botanic notebook filled on the reservation, excluding names of food plants and species not identified, so that no attempt has been made to select in accordance with a preconceived theory. Following the name of each plant are given its uses as described by the Indian doctors, together with its properties as set forth in the United States Dispensatory, one of the leading pharmacopœias in use in this country.[3] For the benefit of those not versed in medical phraseology it may be stated that aperient, cathartic, and deobstruent are terms applied to medicines intended to open or purge the bowels, a diuretic has the property of exciting the flow of urine, a diaphoretic excites perspiration, and a demulcent protects or soothes irritated tissues, while hæmoptysis denotes a peculiar variety of blood-splitting and aphthous is an adjective applied to ulcerations in the mouth.

[3] Wood, T. B., and Bache, F.: Dispensatory of the United States of America, 14th ed., Philadelphia, 1877

SELECTED LIST OF PLANTS USED

1. UNASTE'TSTYÛ = "very small root "--Aristolochia serpentaria--Virginia or black snakeroot: Decoction of root blown upon patient for fever and feverish head ache, and drunk for coughs; root chewed and spit upon wound to cure snake bites; bruised root placed in hollow tooth for toothache, and held against nose made sore by constant blowing in colds. Dispensatory: "A stimulant tonic, acting also as a diaphoretic or diuretic, according to the mode of its application; * * * also been highly recommended in intermittent fevers, and though itself generally inadequate to the cure often proves serviceable as an adjunct to Peruvian bark or sulphate of quinia." Also used for typhous diseases, in dyspepsia, as a gargle for sore throat, as a mild stimulant in typhoid fevers, and to promote eruptions. The genus derives its scientific name from its supposed efficacy in promoting menstrual discharge, and some species have acquired the "reputation of antidotes for the bites of serpents."

2. UNISTIL'Û^{n}ISTÎ[1] = "they stick on"--Cynoglossum Morrisoni--Beggar lice: Decoction of root or top drunk for kidney troubles; bruised root used with bear oil as an ointment for cancer; forgetful persons drink a decoction of this plant, and probably also of other similar bur plants, from an idea that the sticking qualities of the burs will thus be imparted to the memory. From a similar connection of ideas the root is also used in the preparation of love charms. Dispensatory: Not named. C. officinale "has been used as a demulcent and sedative in coughs, catarrh, spitting of blood, dysentery, and diarrhea, and has been also applied externally in bums, ulcers, scrofulous tumors and goiter."

3. Û^{n}NAGÉI = "olack"--Cassia Marilandica--Wild senna: Root bruised and moistened with water for poulticing sores; decoction drunk for fever and for a disease also called û^{n}nage'i, or "black" (same name as plant), in which the hands and eye sockets are said to turn black; also for a disease described as similar to û^{n}nage'i, but more dangerous, in which the eye sockets become black, while black spots appear on the arms, legs, and over the ribs on one side of the body, accompanied by

---

[1] The Cherokee plant names here given are generic names, which are the names commonly used. In many cases the same name is applied to several species and it is only when it is necessary to distinguish between them that the Indians use what might be called specific names. Even then the descriptive term used serves to distinguish only the particular plants under discussion and the introduction of another variety bearing the same generic name would necessitate a new classification of species on a different basis, while hardly any two individuals would classify the species by the same characteristics

partial paralysis, and resulting in death should the black spots appear also on the other side. Dispensatory: Described as "an efficient and safe cathartic, most conveniently given in the form of infusion."

4. KÂSD'ÚTA = "simulating ashes," so called on account of the appearance of the leaves--Gnaphalium decurrens--Life everlasting: Decoction drunk for colds; also used in the sweat bath for various diseases and considered one of their most valuable medical plants. Dispensatory: Not named. Decoctions of two other species of this genus are mentioned as used by country people for chest and bowel diseases, and for hemorrhages, bruises, ulcers, etc., although "probably possessing little medicinal virtue."

5. ALTSA'STI = "a wreath for the head"--Vicia Caroliniana--Vetch: Decoction drunk for dyspepsia and pains in the back, and rubbed on stomach for cramp; also rubbed on ball-players after scratching, to render their muscles tough, and used in the same way after scratching in the disease referred to under $\hat{u}^n$nage'i, in which one side becomes black in spots, with partial paralysis; also used in same manner in decoction with Kâsduta for rheumatism; considered one of their most valuable medicinal herbs. Dispensatory: Not named.

6. DISTAI'YÏ = "they (the roots) are tough"--Tephrosia Virginiana--Catgut, Turkey Pea, Goat's Rue, or Devil's Shoestrings: Decoction drunk for lassitude. Women wash their hair in decoction of its roots to prevent its breaking or falling out, because these roots are very tough and hard to break; from the same idea ball-players rub the decoction on their limbs after scratching, to toughen them. Dispensatory: Described as a cathartic with roots tonic and aperient.

7. U'GA-ATASGI'SKÏ = "the pus oozes out"--Euphorbia hypericifolia--Milkweed: Juice rubbed on for skin eruptions, especially on children's heads; also used as a purgative; decoction drunk for gonorrhœa and similar diseases in both sexes, and held in high estimation for this purpose; juice used as an ointment for sores and for sore nipples, and in connection with other herbs for cancer. Dispensatory: The juice of all of the genus has the property of "powerfully irritating the skin when applied to it," while nearly all are powerful emetics, and cathartics. This species "has been highly commended as a remedy in dysentery after due depletion, diarrhea, menorrhagia, and leucorrhea."

8. GÛ'NÏGWALÏ'SKÏ = "It becomes discolored when bruised"--Scutellaria lateriflora--Skullcap. "The name refers to the red juice which comes out of the stalk when bruised or chewed. A decoction of the four varieties of Gûnigwalï'ski--lateriflora, S. pilosa, Hypericum corymbosum, and Stylosanthes elatior--is drunk to promote menstruation, and the same decoction is also drunk and used as a wash to counteract the ill effects of eating food prepared by a woman in the menstrual condition, or when such a woman by chance comes into a sick room or a house under the tabu; also drunk for diarrhea and used with other herbs in decoction for breast pains. Dispensatory: This plant "produces no very obvious effects," but some doctors regard it as possessed of nervine, antispasmodic and tonic properties. None of the other three species are named.

9. KÂ'GA SKÛ'ⁿTAGÏ = "crow shin"--Adiantum pedatum--Maidenhair Fern: Used either in decoction or poultice for rheumatism and chills, generally in connection with some other fern. The doctors explain that the fronds of the different varieties of fern are curled up in the young plant, but unroll and straighten out as it grows, and consequently a decoction of ferns causes the contracted muscles of the rheumatic patient to unbend and straighten out in like manner. It is also used in decoction for fever. Dispensatory: The leaves "have been supposed to be useful in chronic catarrh and other pectoral affections."

10. ANDA'NKALAGI'SKI = "it removes things from the gums"--Geranium maculatum--Wild Alum, Cranesbill: Used in decoction with Yânû Unihye stï (Vitis cordifolia) to wash the mouths of children in thrush; also used alone for the same purpose by blowing the chewed fiber into the mouth. Dispensatory: "One of our best indigenous astringents. * * * Diarrhea, chronic dysentery, cholora infantum in the latter stages, and the various hemorrhages are the forms of disease in which it is most commonly used." Also valuable as "an application to indolent ulcers, an injection in gleet and leucorrhea, a gargle in relaxation of the uvula and aphthous ulcerations of the throat." The other plant sometimes used with it is not mentioned.

11. Û'ⁿLË, UKÏ'LTÏ = "the locust frequents it"--Gillenia trifoliata--Indian Physic. Two doctors state that it is good as a tea for bowel complaints, with fever and yellow vomit; but another says that it is poisonous and that no decoction is ever drunk, but that the beaten root is a good poultice for swellings. Dispensatory: "Gillenia is a mild and efficient emetic, and like most substances belonging to the same class

occasionally acts upon the bowels. In very small doses it has been thought to be tonic."

12. SKWA'LÏ = Hepatica acutiloba--Liverwort, Heartleaf: Used for coughs either in tea or by chewing root. Those who dream of snakes drink a decoction of this herb and I'natû Ga'n`ka = "snake tongue"-- (Camptosorus rhizophyllus or Walking Fern) to produce vomiting, after which the dreams do not return. The traders buy large quantities of liverwort from the Cherokees, who may thus have learned to esteem it more highly than they otherwise would. The appearance of the other plant, Camptosorus rhizophyllus, has evidently determined its Cherokee name and the use to which it is applied. Dispensatory: "Liverwort is a very mild demulcent tonic and astringent, supposed by some to possess diuretic and deobstruent virtues. It was formerly used in Europe in various complaints, especially chronic hepatic affections, but has fallen into entire neglect. In this country, some years since, it acquired considerable reputation, which, however, it has not maintained as a remedy in hæmoptysis and chronic coughs." The other plant is not named.

13. DA'YEWÛ = "it sews itself up," because the leaves are said to grow together again when torn--Cacalia atriplicifolia--Tassel Flower: Held in great repute as a poultice for cuts, bruises, and cancer, to draw out the blood or poisonous matter. The bruised leaf is bound over the spot and frequently removed. The dry powdered leaf was formerly used to sprinkle over food like salt. Dispensatory--Not named.

14. Â'TALÏ KÛLÏ' = "it climbs the mountain."--Aralia quinquefolia-- Ginseng or "Sang:" Decoction of root drunk for headache, cramps, etc., and for female troubles; chewed root blown on spot for pains in the side. The Cherokees sell large quantities of sang to the traders for 50 cents per pound, nearly equivalent there to two days' wages, a fact which has doubtless increased their idea of its importance. Dispensatory: "The extraordinary medical virtues formerly ascribed to ginseng had no other existence than in the imagination of the Chinese. It is little more than a demulcent, and in this country is not employed as a medicine." The Chinese name, ginseng, is said to refer to the fancied resemblance of the root to a human figure, while in the Cherokee formulas it is addressed as the "great man" or "little man," and this resemblance no doubt has much to do with the estimation in which it is held by both peoples.

15. Û'TSATÏ UWADSÏSKA = "fish scales," from shape of leaves--Thalictrum anemonoides--Meadow Rue: Decoction of root drunk for diarrhea with vomiting. Dispensatory: Not named.

16. K'KWË ULASU'LA = "partridge moccasin"--Cypripedium parviflorum--Ladyslipper: Decoction of root used for worms in children. In the liquid are placed some stalks of the common chickweed or purslane (Cerastium vulgatum) which, from the appearance of its red fleshy stalks, is supposed to have some connection with worms. Dispensatory: Described as "a gentle nervous stimulant" useful in diseases in which the nerves are especially affected. The other herb is not named.

17. A'HAWÏ' AKÄ'TÄ'--"deer eye," from the appearance of the flower-Rudbeckia fulgida--Cone Flower: Decoction of root drunk for flux and for some private diseases; also used as a wash for snakebites and swellings caused by (mythic) tsgâya or worms; also dropped into weak or inflamed eyes. This last is probably from the supposed connection between the eye and the flower resembling the eye. Dispensatory: Not named.

18. UTÏSTUGÏ'--Polygonatum multiflorum latifolium--Solomon's Seal: Root heated and bruised and applied as a poultice to remove an ulcerating swelling called tu'stï', resembling a boil or carbuncle. Dispensatory: This species acts like P. uniflorum, which is said to be emetic, In former times it was used externally in bruises, especially those about the eyes, in tumors, wounds, and cutaneous eruptions and was highly esteemed as a cosmetic. At present it is not employed, though recommended by Hermann as a good remedy in gout and rheumatism." This species in decoction has been found to produce nausea, a cathartic effect and either diaphoresis or diuresis, "and is useful as an internal remedy in piles, and externally in the form of decoction, in the affection of the skin resulting from the poisonous exhalations of certain plants."

19. ÄMÄDITA`TÏ--"water dipper," because water can be sucked up through its hollow stalk--Eupatorium purpureum--Queen of the Meadow, Gravel Root: Root used in decoction with a somewhat similar plant called Ämäditá`tï ü'tanu, or "large water dipper" (not identified) for difficult urination. Dispensatory: "Said to operate as a diuretic. Its vulgar name of gravel root indicates the popular estimation of its

virtues." The genus is described as tonic, diaphoretic, and in large doses emetic and aperient.

20. YÂNA UTSËSTA = "the bear lies on it"--Aspidium acrostichoides-- Shield Fern: Root decoction drunk to produce vomiting, and also used to rub on the skin, after scratching, for rheumatism--in both cases some other plant is added to the decoction; the warm decoction is also held in the mouth to relieve toothache. Dispensatory: Not named.

The results obtained from a careful study of this list maybe summarized as follows: Of the twenty plants described as used by the Cherokees, seven (Nos. 2, 4, 5, 13, 15, 17, and 20) are not noticed in the Dispensatory even in the list of plants sometimes used although regarded as not officinal. It is possible that one or two of these seven plants have medical properties, but this can hardly be true of a larger number unless we are disposed to believe that the Indians are better informed in this regard than the best educated white physicians in the country. Two of these seven plants, however (Nos. 2 and 4), belong to genera which seem to have some of the properties ascribed by the Indians to the species. Five others of the list (Nos. 8, 9, 11, 14, and 16) are used for entirely wrong purposes, taking the Dispensatory as authority, and three of these are evidently used on account of some fancied connection between the plant and the disease, according to the doctrine of signatures. Three of the remainder (Nos. 1, 3, and 6) may be classed as uncertain in their properties, that is, while the plants themselves seem to possess some medical value, the Indian mode of application is so far at variance with recognized methods, or their own statements are so vague and conflicting, that it is doubtful whether any good can result from the use of the herbs. Thus the Unaste'tstiyû, or Virginia Snakeroot, is stated by the Dispensatory to have several uses, and among other things is said to have been highly recommended in intermittent fevers, although alone it is "generally inadequate to the cure." Though not expressly stated, the natural inference is that it must be applied internally, but the Cherokee doctor, while he also uses it for fever, takes the decoction in his mouth and blows it over the head and shoulders of the patient. Another of these, the Distai'yï, or Turkey Pea, is described in the Dispensatory as having roots tonic and aperient. The Cherokees drink a decoction of the roots for a feeling of weakness and languor, from which it might be supposed that they understood the tonic properties of the plant had not the same decoction been used by the women as a hair wash, and by the ball players to bathe their limbs, under the impression that the toughness of the roots would thus be communicated to the hair or muscles. From this fact and from the name of the plant, which means at once hard, tough, or strong, it is quite probable that its roots are believed to give strength to the patient solely because they themselves are so strong and not because they have been proved to be really efficacious. The remaining five plants have generally pronounced medicinal qualities, and are used by the Cherokees for the very purposes for which, according to the Dispensatory, they are best adapted; so that we must admit that so much of their practice is correct, however false the reasoning by which they have arrived at this result.

MEDICAL PRACTICE

Taking the Dispensatory as the standard, and assuming that this list is a fair epitome of what the Cherokees know concerning the medical properties of plants, we find that five plants, or 25 per cent of the whole number, are correctly used; twelve, or 60 per cent, are presumably either worthless or incorrectly used, and three plants, or 15 per cent, are so used that it is difficult to say whether they are of any benefit or not. Granting that two of these three produce good results as used by the Indians, we should have 35 per cent, or about one-third of the whole, as the proportion actually possessing medical virtues, while the remaining two-thirds are inert, if not positively injurious. It is not probable that a larger number of examples would change the proportion to any appreciable extent. A number of herbs used in connection with these principal plants may probably be set down as worthless, inasmuch as they are not named in the Dispensatory.

The results here arrived at will doubtless be a surprise to those persons who hold that an Indian must necessarily be a good doctor, and that the medicine man or conjurer, with his theories of ghosts, witches, and revengeful animals, knows more about the properties of plants and the cure of disease than does the trained botanist or physician who has devoted a lifetime of study to the patient investigation of his specialty, with all the accumulated information contained in the works of his predecessors to build upon, and with all the light thrown upon his pathway by the discoveries of modern science. It is absurd to suppose that the savage, a child in intellect, has reached a higher development in any branch of science than has been attained by the civilized man, the product of long ages of intellectual growth. It would be as unreasonable to suppose that the Indian could be entirely ignorant of the medicinal properties of plants, living as he did in the open air in close communion with nature; but neither in accuracy nor extent can his knowledge be compared for a moment with that of the trained student working upon scientific principles.

Cherokee medicine is an empiric development of the fetich idea. For a disease caused by the rabbit the antidote must be a plant called "rabbit's food," "rabbit's ear," or "rabbit's tail;" for snake dreams the plant used is "snake's tooth;" for worms a plant resembling a worm in appearance, and for inflamed eyes a flower having the appearance and name of "deer's eye." A yellow root must be good when the patient vomits yellow bile, and a black one when dark circles come about his eyes, and in each case the disease and the plant alike are named from the color. A decoction of burs must be a cure for forgetfulness, for there is nothing else that will stick like a bur; and a decoction of the wiry roots of the "devil's shoestrings" must be an efficacious wash to toughen the ballplayer's muscles, for they are almost strong enough to stop the plowshare in the furrow. It must be evident that under such a system the failures must far outnumber the cures, yet it is not so long since half our own medical practice was based upon the same idea of correspondences, for the mediaeval physicians taught that *similia similibus curantur*, and have we not all heard that "the hair of the dog will cure the bite?"

Their ignorance of the true medical principles involved is shown by the regulations prescribed for the patient. With the exception of the fasting, no sanitary precautions are taken to aid in the recovery of the sick man or to contribute to his comfort. Even the fasting is as much religious as sanative, for in most cases where it is prescribed the doctor also must abstain from food until sunset, just as in the Catholic church both priest and communicants remain fasting from midnight until after the celebration of the divine mysteries. As the Indian cuisine is extremely limited, no delicate or appetizing dishes are prepared for the patient, who partakes of the same heavy, sodden cornmeal dumplings and bean bread which form his principal food in health. In most cases certain kinds of food are prohibited, such as squirrel meat, fish, turkey, etc.; but the reason is not that such food is considered deleterious to health, as we understand it, but because of some fanciful connection with the disease spirit. Thus if squirrels have caused the illness the patient must not eat squirrel meat. If the disease be rheumatism, he must not eat the leg of any animal, because the limbs are generally the seat of this malady. Lye, salt, and hot food are always forbidden when there is any prohibition at all; but here again, in nine cases out of ten, the regulation, instead of being beneficial, serves only to add to his discomfort. Lye enters into almost all the food preparations of the Cherokees, the alkaline potash taking the place of salt, which is seldom used among them, having been introduced by the whites. Their bean and chestnut bread, cornmeal dumplings' hominy, and gruel are all boiled in a pot, all contain lye, and are all, excepting the last, served up hot from the fire. When cold their bread is about as hard and tasteless as a lump of yesterday's dough, and to condemn a sick man to a diet of such dyspeptic food, eaten cold without even a pinch of salt to give it a relish, would seem to be sufficient to kill him with, out any further aid from the doctor. The salt or lye so strictly prohibited is really a tonic and appetizer, and in many diseases acts with curative effect. So much for the health regimen.

In serious cases the patient is secluded and no strangers are allowed to enter the house. On first thought this would appear to be a genuine sanitary precaution for the purpose of securing rest and quiet to the sick man. Such, however, is not the case. The necessity for quiet has probably never occurred to the Cherokee doctor, and this regulation is intended simply to prevent any direct or indirect contact with a woman in a pregnant or menstrual condition. Among all primitive nations, including the ancient Hebrews, we find an elaborate code of rules in regard to the conduct and treatment of women on arriving at the age of puberty, during pregnancy and the menstrual periods, and at childbirth. Among the Cherokees the presence of a woman under any of these conditions, or even the presence of any one who has come from a house where such a woman resides, is considered to neutralize all the effects of the doctor's treatment. For this reason all women, excepting those of the household, are excluded. A man is forbidden to enter, because he may have had intercourse with a tabued woman, or may have come in contact with her in some other way; and children also are shut out, because they may have come from a cabin where dwells a woman subject to exclusion. What is supposed to be the effect of the presence of a menstrual woman in the family of the patient is not clear; but judging from analogous customs in other tribes and from rules still enforced among the Cherokees, notwithstanding their long contact with the whites, it seems probable that in former times the patient was removed to a smaller house or temporary bark lodge built for his accommodation whenever the tabu as to women was prescribed by the doctor. Some of the old men assert that in former times sick persons were removed to the public townhouse, where they remained under the care of the doctors until they either recovered or died. A curious instance of this prohibition is given in the second Didûⁿlë'skï (rheumatism) formula from the Gahuni manuscript (see page 350), where the patient is required to abstain from touching a squirrel, a dog, a cat, a mountain trout, or a woman, and must also have a chair appropriated to his use alone during the four days that he is under treatment.

In cases of the children's disease known as Gûⁿwani'gista'ï (see formulas) it is forbidden to carry the child outdoors, but this is not to procure rest for the little one, or to guard against exposure to cold air, but because the birds send this disease, and should a bird chance to be flying by overhead at the moment the flapping of its wings would fan the disease back into the body of the patient.

ILLUSTRATION OF THE TABU

On a second visit to the reservation the writer once had a practical illustration of the gaktû'ⁿata or tabu, which may be of interest as showing how little sanitary ideas have to do with these precautions. Having received several urgent invitations from Tsiskwa (Bird), an old shaman of considerable repute, who was anxious to talk, but confined to his bed by sickness, it was determined to visit him at his house, several miles distant.

On arriving we found another doctor named Sû'ⁿkï (The Mink) in charge of the patient and were told that he had just that morning begun a four days' gaktûⁿta, which, among other provisions, excluded all visitors. It was of no use to argue that we had come by the express request of Tsiskwa.

The laws of the gaktûⁿta were as immutable as those of the Medes and Persians, and neither doctor nor patient could hope for favorable results from the treatment unless the regulations were enforced to the letter. But although we might not enter the house; there was no reason why we should not talk to the old man, so seats were placed for us outside the door, while Tsiskwa lay stretched out on the bed just inside and The Mink perched himself on the fence a few yards distant to keep an eye on the proceedings. As there was a possibility that a white man might unconsciously affect the operation of the Indian medicine, the writer deemed it advisable to keep out of sight altogether, and accordingly took up a position just around the corner of the house, but within easy hearing distance, while the interpreter sat facing the doorway within a few feet of the sick man inside. Then began an animated conversation, Tsiskwa inquiring, through the interpreter, as to the purpose of the Government in gathering such information, wanting to know how we had succeeded with other shamans and asking various questions in regard to other tribes and their customs.

The replies were given in the same manner, an attempt being also made to draw him out as to the extent of his own knowledge. Thus we talked until the old man grew weary, but throughout the whole of this singular interview neither party saw the other, nor was the gaktûⁿta violated by entering the house. From this example it must be sufficiently evident that the tabu as to visitors is not a hygienic precaution for securing greater quiet to the patient, or to prevent the spread of contagion, but that it is simply a religious observance of the tribe, exactly parallel to many of the regulations among the ancient Jews, as laid down in the book of Leviticus.

———————◆———————

NEGLECT OF SANITARY REGULATIONS

No rules are ever formulated as to fresh air or exercise, for the sufficient reason that the door of the Cherokee log cabin is always open, excepting at night and on the coldest days in winter, while the Indian is seldom in the house during his waking hours unless when necessity compels him. As most of their cabins are still built in the old Indian style, without windows, the open door furnishes the only means by which light is admitted to the interior, although when closed the fire on the hearth helps to make amends for the deficiency. On the other hand, no precautions are taken to guard against cold, dampness, or sudden drafts. During the greater part of the year whole families sleep outside upon the ground, rolled up in an old blanket. The Cherokee is careless of exposure and utterly indifferent to the simplest rules of hygiene. He will walk all day in a pouring rain clad only in a thin shirt and a pair of pants. He goes barefoot and frequently bareheaded nearly the entire year, and even on a frosty morning in late November, when the streams are of almost icy coldness, men and women will deliberately ford the river where the water is waist deep in preference to going a few hundred yards to a foot-log. At their dances in the open air men, women, and children, with bare feet and thinly clad, dance upon the damp ground from darkness until daylight, sometimes enveloped in a thick mountain fog which makes even the neighboring treetops invisible, while the mothers have their infants laid away under the bushes with only a shawl between them and the cold ground. In their ball plays also each young man, before going into the game, is subjected to an ordeal of dancing, bleeding, and cold plunge baths, without food or sleep, which must unquestionably waste his physical energy.

In the old days when the Cherokee was the lord of the whole country from the Savannah to the Ohio, well fed and warmly clad and leading an active life in the open air, he was able to maintain a condition of robust health notwithstanding the incorrectness of his medical ideas and his general disregard of sanitary regulations. But with the advent of the white man and the destruction of the game all this was changed. The East Cherokee of to-day is a dejected being; poorly fed, and worse clothed, rarely tasting meat, cut off from the old free life, and with no incentive to a better, and constantly bowed down by a sense of helpless degradation in the presence of his conqueror. Considering all the circumstances, it may seem a matter of surprise that any of them are still in existence. As a matter of fact, the best information that could be obtained in the absence of any official statistics indicated a slow but steady decrease during the last five years. Only the constitutional vigor, inherited from their warrior ancestors, has enabled them to sustain the shock of the changed conditions of the last half century. The uniform good health of the children in the training school shows that the case is not hopeless, however, and that under favorable conditions, with a proper food supply and a regular mode of living, the Cherokee can hold his own with the white man.

THE SWEAT BATH-BLEEDING--RUBBING--BATHING

In addition to their herb treatment the Cherokees frequently resort to sweat baths, bleeding, rubbing, and cold baths in the running stream, to say nothing of the beads and other conjuring paraphernalia generally used in connection with the ceremony. The sweat bath was in common use among almost all the tribes north of Mexico excepting the central and eastern Eskimo, and was considered the great cure-all in sickness and invigorant in health. Among many tribes it appears to have been regarded as a ceremonial observance, but the Cherokees seem to have looked upon it simply as a medical application, while the ceremonial part was confined to the use of the plunge bath. The person wishing to make trial of the virtues of the sweat bath entered the â'sï, a small earth-covered log house only high enough to allow of sitting down. After divesting himself of his clothing, some large bowlders, previously heated in a fire, were placed near him, and over them was poured a decoction of the beaten roots of the wild parsnip. The door was closed so that no air could enter from the outside, and the patient sat in the sweltering steam until he was in a profuse perspiration and nearly choked by the pungent fumes of the decoction. In accordance with general Indian practice it may be that he plunged into the river before resuming his clothing; but in modern times this part of the operation is omitted and the patient is drenched with cold water instead. Since the âsï has gone out of general use the sweating takes place in the ordinary dwelling, the steam being confined under a blanket wrapped around the patient. During the prevalence of the smallpox epidemic among the Cherokees at the close of the late war the sweat bath was universally called into requisition to stay the progress of the disease, and as the result about three hundred of the band died, while many of the survivors will carry the marks of the visitation to the grave. The sweat bath, with the accompanying cold water application, being regarded as the great panacea, seems to have been resorted to by the Indians in all parts of the country whenever visited by smallpox--originally introduced by the whites--and in consequence of this mistaken treatment they have died, in the language of an old writer, "like rotten sheep" and at times whole tribes have been almost swept away. Many of the Cherokees tried to ward off the disease by eating the flesh of the buzzard, which they believe to enjoy entire immunity from sickness, owing to its foul smell, which keeps the disease spirits at a distance.

Bleeding is resorted to in a number of cases, especially in rheumatism and in preparing for the ball play. There are two methods of performing the operation, bleeding proper and scratching, the latter being preparatory to rubbing on the medicine, which is thus brought into more direct contact with the blood. The bleeding is performed with a small cupping horn, to which suction is applied in the ordinary manner, after scarification with a flint or piece of broken glass. In the blood thus drawn out the shaman claims sometimes to find a minute pebble, a sharpened stick or something of the kind, which he asserts to be the cause of the trouble and to have been conveyed into the body of the patient through the evil spells of an enemy. He frequently pretends to suck out such an object by the application of the lips alone, without any scarification whatever. Scratching is a painful process and is performed with a brier, a flint arrowhead, a rattlesnake's tooth, or even with a piece of glass, according to the nature of the ailment, while in preparing the young men for the ball play the shaman uses an instrument somewhat resembling a comb, having seven teeth made from the sharpened splinters of the leg bone of a turkey. The scratching is usually done according to a particular pattern, the regular method for the ball play being to draw the scratcher four times down the upper part of each arm, thus making twenty-eight scratches each about 6 inches in length, repeating the operation on each arm below the elbow and on each leg above and below the knee. Finally, the instrument is drawn across the breast from the two shoulders so as to form a cross; another curving stroke is made to connect the two upper ends of the cross, and the same pattern is repeated on the back, so that the body is thus gashed in nearly three hundred places. Although very painful for a while, as may well be supposed, the scratches do not penetrate deep enough to result seriously, excepting in some cases where erysipelas sets in. While the blood is still flowing freely the medicine, which in this case is intended to toughen the muscles of the player, is rubbed into the wounds after which the sufferer plunges into the stream and washes off the blood. In order that the blood may flow the longer without clotting it is frequently scraped off with a small switch as it flows. In rheumatism and other local diseases the scratching is confined to the part affected. The instrument used is selected in accordance with the mythologic theory, excepting in the case of the piece of glass, which is merely a modern makeshift for the flint arrowhead.

Rubbing, used commonly for pains and swellings of the abdomen, is a very simple operation performed with the tip of the finger or the palm of the hand, and can not be dignified with the name of massage. In one of the Gahuni formulas for treating snake bites (page 351) the operator is told to rub in a direction contrary to that in which the snake coils itself, because "this is just the same as uncoiling it." Blowing upon the part affected, as well as upon the head, hands, and other parts of the body, is also an important feature of the ceremonial performance. In one of the formulas it is specified that the doctor must blow first upon the right hand of the patient, then upon the left foot, then upon the left hand, and finally upon the right foot, thus making an imaginary cross.

Bathing in the running stream, or "going to water," as it is called, is one of their most frequent medico-religious ceremonies, and is performed on a great variety of occasions, such as at each new moon, before eating the new food at the green corn dance, before the medicine dance and other ceremonial dances before and after the ball play, in connection with the prayers for long life, to counteract the effects of bad dreams or the evil spells of an enemy, and as a part of the regular treatment in various diseases. The details of the ceremony are very elaborate and vary according to the purpose for which it is performed, but in all cases both shaman and client are fasting from the previous evening, the ceremony being generally performed just at daybreak. The bather usually dips completely under the water four or seven times, but in some cases it is sufficient to pour the water from the hand upon the head and breast. In the ball play the ball sticks are dipped into the water at the same time. While the bather is in the water the shaman is going through with his part of the performance on the bank and draws omens from the motion of the beads between his thumb and finger, or of the fishes in the water. Although the old customs are fast dying out this ceremony is never neglected at the ball play, and is also strictly observed by many families on occasion of eating the new corn, at each new moon, and on other special occasions, even when it is necessary to break the ice in the stream for the purpose, and to the neglect of this rite the older people attribute many of the evils which have come upon the tribe in later days. The latter part of autumn is deemed the most suitable season of the year for this ceremony, as the leaves which then cover the surface of the stream are supposed to impart their medicinal virtues to the water.

SHAMANS AND WHITE PHYSICIANS

Of late years, especially since the establishment of schools among them, the Cherokees are gradually beginning to lose confidence in the abilities of their own doctors and are becoming more disposed to accept treatment from white physicians. The shamans are naturally jealous of this infringement upon their authority and endeavor to prevent the spread of the heresy by asserting the convenient doctrine that the white man's medicine is inevitably fatal to an Indian unless eradicated from the system by a continuous course of treatment for four years under the hands of a skillful shaman.

The officers of the training school established by the Government a few years ago met with considerable difficulty on this account for some time, as the parents insisted on removing the children at the first appearance of illness in order that they might be treated by the shamans, until convinced by experience that the children received better attention at the school than could possibly be had in their own homes. In one instance, where a woman was attacked by a pulmonary complaint akin to consumption, her husband, a man of rather more than the usual amount of intelligence, was persuaded to call in the services of a competent white physician, who diagnosed the case and left a prescription.

On a second visit, a few days later, he found that the family, dreading the consequences of this departure from old customs, had employed a shaman, who asserted that the trouble was caused by a sharpened stick which some enemy bad caused to be imbedded in the woman's side. He accordingly began a series of conjurations for the removal of the stick, while the white physician and his medicine were disregarded, and in due time the woman died.

Two children soon followed her to the grave, from the contagion or the inherited seeds of the same disease, but here also the sharpened sticks were held responsible, and, notwithstanding the three deaths under such treatment, the husband and father, who was at one time a preacher still has faith in the assertions of the shaman. The appointment of a competent physician to look after the health of the Indians would go far to eradicate these false ideas and prevent much sickness and suffering; but, as the Government has made no such provision, the Indians, both on and off the reservation, excepting the children in the home school, are entirely without medical care.

MEDICINE DANCES

The Cherokees have a dance known as the Medicine Dance, which is generally performed in connection with other dances when a number of people assemble for a night of enjoyment. It possesses no features of special interest and differs in no essential respect from a dozen other of the lesser dances. Besides this, however, there was another, known as the Medicine Boiling Dance, which, for importance and solemn ceremonial, was second only to the great Green Corn Dance. It has now been discontinued on the reservation for about twenty years. It took place in the fall, probably preceding the Green Corn Dance, and continued four days. The principal ceremony in connection with it was the drinking of a strong decoction of various herbs, which acted as a violent emetic and purgative. The usual fasting and going to water accompanied the dancing and medicine-drinking.

DESCRIPTION OF SYMPTOMS

It is exceedingly difficult to obtain from the doctors any accurate statement of the nature of a malady, owing to the fact that their description of the symptoms is always of the vaguest character, while in general the name given to the disease by the shaman expresses only his opinion as to the occult cause of the trouble. Thus they have definite names for rheumatism, toothache, boils, and a few other ailments of like positive character, but beyond this their description of symptoms generally resolves itself into a statement that the patient has bad dreams, looks black around the eyes, or feels tired, while the disease is. assigned such names as "when they dream of snakes," "when they dream of fish," "when ghosts trouble them," "when something is making something else eat them," or "when the food is changed," i.e., when a witch causes it to sprout and grow in the body of the patient or transforms it into a lizard, frog, or sharpened stick.

THE PAY OF THE SHAMAN

The consideration which the doctor receives for his services is called ugista'`tï, a word of doubtful etymology, but probably derived from the verb tsï'giû, "I take" or "I eat." In former times this was generally a deer-skin or a pair of moccasins, but is now a certain quantity of cloth, a garment, or a handkerchief. The shamans disclaim the idea that the ugista'`tï is pay, in our sense of the word, but assert that it is one of the agencies in the removal and banishment of the disease spirit. Their explanation is somewhat obscure, but the cloth seems to be intended either as an offering to the disease spirit, as a ransom to procure the release of his intended victim, or as a covering to protect the hand of a shaman while engaged in pulling the disease from the body of the patient. The first theory, which includes also the idea of vicarious atonement, is common to many primitive peoples. Whichever maybe the true explanation, the evil influence of the disease is believed to enter into the cloth, which must therefore be sold or given away by the doctor, as otherwise it will cause his death when the pile thus accumulating reaches the height of his head. No evil results seem to follow its transfer from the shaman to a third party. The doctor can not bestow anything thus received upon a member of his own family unless that individual gives him something in return. If the consideration thus received, however, be anything eatable, the doctor may partake along with the rest of the family. As a general rule the doctor makes no charge for his services, and the consideration is regarded as a free-will offering. This remark applies only to the medical practice, as the shaman always demands and receives a fixed remuneration for performing love charms, hunting ceremonials, and other conjurations of a miscellaneous character. Moreover, whenever the beads are used the patient must furnish a certain quantity of new cloth upon which to place them, and at the close of the ceremony the doctor rolls up the cloth, beads and all, and takes them away with him. The cloth thus received by the doctor for working with the beads must not be used by him, but must be sold. In one instance a doctor kept a handkerchief which he received for his services, but instead sold a better one of his own. Additional cloth is thus given each time the ceremony is repeated, each time a second four days' course of treatment is begun, and as often as the doctor sees fit to change his method of procedure. Thus, when he begins to treat a sick man for a disease caused by rabbits, he expects to receive a certain ugista'`tï; but, should he decide after a time that the terrapin or the red bird is responsible for the, trouble, he adopts a different course of treatment, for which another ugista''tï is necessary. Should the sickness not yield readily to his efforts, it is because the disease animal requires a greater ugista''tï, and the quantity of cloth must be doubled, so that on the whole the doctrine is a very convenient one for the shaman. In many of the formulas explicit directions are given as to the pay which the shaman is to receive for performing the ceremony. In one of the Gatigwanasti formulas, after specifying the amount of cloth to be paid, the writer of it makes the additional proviso that it must be "pretty good cloth, too," asserting as a clincher that "this is what the old folks said a long time ago."

The ugista''tï can not be paid by either one of a married couple to the other, and, as it is considered a necessary accompaniment of the application, it follows that a shaman can not treat his own wife in sickness, and vice versa. Neither can the husband or wife of the sick person send for the doctor, but the call must come from some one of the blood relatives of the patient. In one instance within the writer's knowledge a woman complained that her husband was very sick and needed a doctor's attention, but his relatives were taking no steps in the matter and it was not permissible for her to do so.

CEREMONIES FOR GATHERING PLANTS AND PREPARING MEDICINE

There are a number of ceremonies and regulations observed in connection with the gathering of the herbs, roots, and barks, which can not be given in detail within the limits of this paper. In searching for his medicinal plants the shaman goes provided with a number of white and red beads, and approaches the plant from a certain direction, going round it from right to left one or four times, reciting certain prayers the while. He then pulls up the plant by the roots and drops one of the beads into the hole and covers it up with the loose earth. In one of the formulas for hunting ginseng the hunter addresses the mountain as the "Great Man" and assures it that he comes only to take a small piece of flesh (the ginseng) from its side, so that it seems probable that the bead is intended as a compensation to the earth for the plant thus torn from her bosom. In some cases the doctor must pass by the first three plants met until he comes to the fourth, which he takes and may then return for the others. The bark is always taken from the east side of the tree, and when the root or branch is used it must also be one which runs out toward the east, the reason given being that these have imbibed more medical potency from the rays of the sun.

When the roots, herbs, and barks which enter into the prescription have been thus gathered the doctor ties them up into a convenient package, which he takes to a running stream and casts into the water with appropriate prayers. Should the package float, as it generally does, he accepts the fact as an omen that his treatment will be successful. On the other band, should it sink, he concludes that some part of the preceding ceremony has been improperly carried out and at once sets about procuring a new package, going over the whole performance from the beginning. Herb-gathering by moonlight, so important a feature in European folk medicine, seems to be no part of Cherokee ceremonial. There are fixed regulations in regard to the preparing of the decoction, the care of the medicine during the continuance of the treatment, and the disposal of what remains after the treatment is at an end. In the arrangement of details the shaman frequently employs the services of a lay assistant. Id these degenerate days a number of upstart pretenders to the healing art have arisen in the tribe and endeavor to impose upon the ignorance of their fellows by posing as doctors, although knowing next to nothing of the prayers and ceremonies, without which there can be no virtue in the application. These impostors are sternly frowned down and regarded with the utmost contempt by the real professors, both men and women, who have been initiated into the sacred mysteries and proudly look upon themselves as conservators of the ancient ritual of the past.

THE CHEROKEE GODS AND THEIR ABIDING PLACES

After what has been said in elucidation of the theories involved in the medical formulas, the most important and numerous of the series, but little remains to be added in regard to the others, beyond what is contained in the explanation accompanying each one. A few points, however, may be briefly noted.

The religion of the Cherokees, like that of most of our North American tribes, is zootheism or animal worship, with the survival of that earlier stage designated by Powell as hecastotheism, or the worship of all things tangible, and the beginnings of a higher system in which the elements and the great powers of nature are deified. Their pantheon includes gods in the heaven above, on the earth beneath, and in the waters under the earth, but of these the animal gods constitute by far the most numerous class, although the elemental gods are more important. Among the animal gods insects and fishes occupy a subordinate place, while quadrupeds, birds, and reptiles are invoked almost constantly. The uktena (a mythic great horned serpent), the rattlesnake, and the terrapin, the various species of hawk, and the rabbit, the squirrel, and the dog are the principal animal gods. The importance of the god bears no relation to the size of the animal, and in fact the larger animals are but seldom invoked. The spider also occupies a prominent place in the love and life-destroying formulas, his duty being to entangle the soul of his victim in the meshes of his web or to pluck it from the body of the doomed man and drag it way to the black coffin in the Darkening Land.

Among what may be classed as elemental gods the principal are fire, water, and the sun, all of which are addressed under figurative names. The sun is called Une`'lanû'hï, "the apportioner," just as our word moon means originally "the measurer." Indians and Aryans alike, having noticed how these great luminaries divide and measure day and night, summer and winter, with never varying regularity, have given to each a name which should indicate these characteristics, thus showing how the human mind constantly moves on along the same channels. Missionaries have naturally, but incorrectly, assumed this apportioner of all things to be the suppositional "Great Spirit" of the Cherokees and hence the word is used in the Bible translation as synonymous with God. In ordinary conversation and in the lesser myths the sun is called Nû'ntâ. The sun is invoked chiefly by the ball-player, while the hunter prays to the fire; but every important ceremony--whether connected with medicine, love, hunting, or the ball play--contains a prayer to the "Long Person," the formulistic name for water, or, more strictly speaking, for the river. The wind, the storm, the cloud, and the frost are also invoked in different formulas.

But few inanimate gods are included in the category, the principal being the Stone, to which the shaman prays while endeavoring to find a lost article by means of a swinging pebble suspended by a string; the Flint, invoked when the shaman is about to scarify the patient with a flint arrow-head before rubbing on the medicine; and the Mountain, which is addressed in one or two of the formulas thus far translated. Plant gods do not appear prominently, the chief one seeming to be the ginseng, addressed in the formulas as the "Great Man" or "Little Man," although its proper Cherokee name signifies the "Mountain Climber."

A number of personal deities are also invoked, the principal being the Red Man. He is one of the greatest of the gods, being repeatedly called upon in formulas of all kinds, and is hardly subordinate to the Fire, the Water, or the Sun. His identity is as yet uncertain, but he seems to be intimately connected with the Thunder family. In a curious marginal note in one of the Gahuni formulas (page 350), it is stated that when the patient is a woman the doctor must pray to the Red Man, but when treating a man he must pray to the Red Woman, so that this personage seems to have dual sex characteristics. Another god invoked in the hunting songs is Tsu'l`kalû', or "Slanting Eyes" (see Cherokee Myths), a giant hunter who lives in one of the great mountains of the Blue Ridge and owns all the game. Others are the Little Men, probably the two Thunder boys; the Little People, the fairies who live in the rock cliffs; and even the De'tsata, a diminutive sprite who holds the place of our Puck. One unwritten formula, which could not be obtained correctly by dictation, was addressed to the "Red-Headed Woman, whose hair hangs down to the ground."

The personage invoked is always selected in accordance with the theory of the formula and the duty to be performed. Thus, when a sickness is caused by a fish, the Fish-hawk, the Heron, or some other fish-eating bird is implored to come and seize the intruder and destroy it, so that the patient may find relief. When the trouble is caused by a worm or an insect, some insectivorous bird is called in for the same purpose. When a flock of redbirds is pecking at the vitals of the sick man the Sparrow-hawk is brought down to scatter them, and when the rabbit, the great mischief-maker, is the evil genius, he is driven out by the Rabbit-hawk. Sometimes after the intruder has been thus expelled "a small portion still remains," in the words of the formula, and accordingly the Whirlwind is called down from the treetops to carry the remnant to the uplands and there scatter it so that it shall never reappear. The hunter prays to the fire, from which he draws his omens; to the reed, from which he makes his arrows; to Tsu'l`kalû, the great lord of the game, and finally addresses in songs the very animals which he intends to kill. The lover prays to the Spider to hold fast the affections of his beloved one in the meshes of his web, or to the Moon, which looks down upon him in the dance. The warrior prays to the Red War-club, and the man about to set out on a dangerous expedition prays to the Cloud to envelop him and conceal him from his enemies.

Each spirit of good or evil has its distinct and appropriate place of residence. The Rabbit is declared to live in the broomsage on the hillside, the Fish dwells in a bend of the river under the pendant hemlock branches, the Terrapin lives in the great pond in the West, and the Whirlwind abides in the leafy treetops. Each disease animal, when driven away from his prey by some more powerful animal, endeavors to find shelter in his accustomed haunt. It must be stated here that the animals of the formulas are not the ordinary, everyday animals, but their great progenitors, who live in the upper world (galû'^{n}lati) above the arch of the firmament.

COLOR SYMBOLISM

Color symbolism plays an important part in the shamanistic system of the Cherokees, no less than in that of other tribes. Each one of the cardinal points has its corresponding color and each color its symbolic meaning, so that each spirit invoked corresponds in color and local habitation with the characteristics imputed to him, and is connected with other spirits of the same name, but of other colors, living in other parts of the upper world and differing widely in their characteristics. Thus the Red Man, living in the east, is the spirit of power, triumph, and success, but the Black Man, in the West, is the spirit of death. The shaman therefore invokes the Red Man to the assistance of his client and consigns his enemy to the fatal influences of the Black Man.

The symbolic color system of the Cherokees, which will be explained more fully in connection with the formulas, is as follows:

East	red	success; triumph.
North	blue	defeat; trouble.
West	black	death.
South	white	peace; happiness.
Above?	brown	unascertained, but propitious.
---------	yellow	about the same as blue.

There is a great diversity in the color systems of the various tribes, both as to the location and significance of the colors, but for obvious reasons black was generally taken as the symbol of death, while white and red signified, respectively, peace and war. It is somewhat remarkable that red was the emblem of power and triumph among the ancient Oriental nations no less than among the modern Cherokees.[1]

[1] For more in regard to color symbolism, see Mallery's Pictographs of the North American Indians in Fourth Report of the Bureau of Ethnology, pp. 53-57, Washington, 1886; Gatschet's Creek Migration Legend, vol. 2, pp. 31-41, St. Louis, 1888; Brinton's Kiche Myths in Proceedings of the American Philosophical Society, vol. 19, pp. 646-647, Philadelphia, 1882

IMPORTANCE ATTACHED TO NAMES

In many of the formulas, especially those relating to love and to life-destroying, the shaman mentions the name and clan of his client, of the intended victim, or of the girl whose affections it is desired to win. The Indian regards his name, not as a mere label, but as a distinct part of his personality, just as much as are his eyes or his teeth, and believes that injury will result as surely from the malicious handling of his name as from a wound inflicted on any part of his physical organism. This belief was found among the various tribes from the Atlantic to the Pacific, and has occasioned a number of curious regulations in regard to the concealment and change of names. It may be on this account that both Powhatan and Pocahontas are known in history under assumed appellations, their true names having been concealed from the whites until the pseudonyms were too firmly established to be supplanted. Should his prayers have no apparent effect when treating a patient for some serious illness, the shaman sometimes concludes that the name is affected, and accordingly goes to water, with appropriate ceremonies, and christens the patient with a new name, by which he is henceforth to be known. He then begins afresh, repeating the formulas with the new name selected for the patient, in the confident hope that his efforts will be crowned with success.

LANGUAGE OF THE FORMULAS

A few words remain to be said in regard to the language of the formulas. They are full of archaic and figurative expressions, many of which are unintelligible to the common people, and some of which even the shamans themselves are now unable to. explain. These archaic forms, like the old words used by our poets, lend a peculiar beauty which can hardly be rendered in a translation. They frequently throw light on the dialectic evolution of the language, as many words found now only in the nearly extinct Lower Cherokee dialect occur in formulas which in other respects are written in the Middle or Upper dialect. The R sound, the chief distinguishing characteristic of the old Lower dialect, of course does not occur, as there are no means of indicating it in the Cherokee syllabary. Those who are accustomed to look to the Bible for all beauty in sacred expression will be surprised to find that these formulas abound in the loftiest flights of poetic imagery.

This is especially true of the prayers used to win the love of a woman or to destroy the life of an enemy, in which we find such expressions as--"Now your soul fades away--your spirit shall grow less and dwindle away, never to reappear;" "Let her be completely veiled in loneliness--O Black Spider, may you hold her soul in your web, so that it may never get through the meshes;" and the final declaration of the lover, "Your soul has come into the very center of my soul, never to turn away."

In the translation it has been found advisable to retain as technical terms a few words which could not well be rendered literally, such as ada'wëhï and ugistâ`tï.

These words will be found explained in the proper place. Transliterations of the Cherokee text of the formulas are given, but it must be distinctly understood that the translations are intended only as free renderings of the spirit of the originals, exact translations with grammatic and glossarial notes being deferred until a more extended study of the language has been made, when it is hoped to present with more exactness of detail the whole body of the formulas, of which the specimens here given are but a small portion.

The facsimile formulas are copies from the manuscripts now in possession of the Bureau of Ethnology, and the portraits are from photographs taken by the author in the field.

NOTE ON THE ORTHOGRAPHY AND TRANSLATION

In the Cherokee text both d and g have a medial sound, approximating the sounds of *t* and *k* respectively. The other letters are pronounced in regular accordance with the alphabet of the Bureau of Ethnology. The language abounds in nasal and aspirate sounds, the most difficult of the latter being the aspirate `l`, which to one familiar only with English sounds like *tl*.

A few words whose meaning could not be satisfactorily ascertained have been distinctively indicated in the Cherokee text by means of italics. In the translation the corresponding expression has been queried, or the space left entirely blank. On examining the text the student can not fail to be struck by the great number of verbs ending in *iga*. This is a peculiar form hardly ever used excepting in these formulas, where almost every paragraph contains one or more such verbs. It implies that the subject has just come and is now performing the action, and that he came for that purpose. In addition to this, many of these verbs may be either assertive or imperative (expressing entreaty), according to the accent. Thus *hatû'ⁿ-gani'ga* means "you have just come and are listening and it is for that purpose you came." By slightly accenting the final syllable it becomes "come at once to listen." It will thus be seen that the great majority of the formulas are declarative rather than petitional in form-laudatory rhapsodies instead of prayers, in the ordinary sense of the word.

FORMULA FOR TREATING THE CRIPPLER (RHEUMATISM)

MEDICINE.

DIDÛⁿLË'SKÏ ADANÛⁿ'WÂTÏ KANÂHË'SKÏ.

Sgë! Ha-Nûⁿdûgiû'ⁿyï tsûl`dâ'histï, Gi`lï Gigage'ï, hanâ'gwa hatû'ⁿgani'ga usïnuli'yu. Hida'wëhi-gâgû', gahu'stï tsan'ultï nige'sûⁿna. Ha-diskwûlti'yû tï'nanugagï', ase'gwû nige'sûⁿna tsagista`'tï adûⁿni'ga. Ulsg'eta hûⁿhihyû'ⁿstani'ga. Ha-usdig'iyu-gwû ha-e'la-wastû'ⁿ iyû'ⁿta dûhilâ'hïstani'ga.

Sgë! Ha-Uhûⁿtsâ'yï tsûl`dâ'histï Gi`lï Sa`ka'nï, hanâ'gwa ha-tû'ⁿgani'ga usïnuli'yu. Hida'wëhi-gâgû', gahu'stï tsanu'ltï nige'sûⁿna. Diskwûlti'yû ti'nanugai', ase'gwû nige'sûⁿna tsagista`'tï adûⁿni'ga. Ulsge'ta hûⁿhihyûⁿstani'ga, Ha-usdigi'yu-gwû ha-e'la-wastû'ⁿ iyû'ta dûhitâ'hïstani'ga.

Sgë! (Ha)-Usûhi'(-yï) tsûl`dâ'histï, Gi`l'ï Gûnⁿage'ï, hanâ'gwa hatû'ⁿgani'ga usïnuli'yû. Hida'wëhi-gâgû', gahu'sti tsanu'ltï nige'sû'ⁿna. Diskwûlti'yû tinanugagï', ase'gwû nige'sûⁿna tsagista`'tï adûⁿni'ga. Ulsg'eta hûⁿhihyûⁿstani'ga. Ha-usdigi'yu-gwû ha-e'la-wastû'ⁿ iyû'ⁿta dûhitâ'hïstani'ga.

Sgë! Wa'halä' tsûl`dâ'histï, Gi'`lï Tsûne'ga, hanâ'gwa hatû'ⁿgani'ga usïliuli'yu. Hida'wëhi-gâgû', gahu'stï tsanû'ltï nige'sûⁿna. Diskwûlti'yû ti'nanugagï', ase'gwû nige'sûⁿna tsagista`'tï adûⁿni'ga. Ha-ulsge'ta hûⁿhihyû'ⁿstani'ga. Ha-usdigi'yu-gwû e'lawastû'ⁿ iyû'ⁿta dûhità'hïstani'ga.

Sgë! Wa'halä tsûl`dâ'histï Tû'ksï Tsûne'ga, hanâ'gwa hatû'ⁿgani'ga usïnuli'yu. Hida'wëhi-gâgû', gahu'stï tsanu'ltï nige'sûⁿna. Ha-kâ'lû *gayûske'la* tsatûⁿ'neli'ga. Utsïna'wa nulatänûⁿta.

(Degâsisisgû'ⁿï.)--Tûksï uhya'ska gûnsta`tï' na'skï igahi'ta gûnstâ'ï hï'skï iyuntale'gï tsûntûngi'ya. Ûⁿskwû'ta kïlû' atsâ'tastï sâ'gwa iyûtsâ'tastï, nû'`kï igû'ⁿkta`tï, naski-gwû' diûⁿlë'nïskâhï' igû'ⁿyi'yï tsale'nihû. Nû'`kine ûⁿskwû'ta kïlû' nû'`kï iyatsâ'tastï. Uhyaska'hi-`nû ade'la degû`laï tä'lï unine'ga-gwû' nû'ⁿwâti-`nû' higûnehâ'ï uhyaskâ'hï usdi'a-gwû. Une'lagi-`nû sâï' agadâ'ï agadi'dï û'ⁿti-gwû' yïkï' âsi'yu-gwû na'ski-`nû aganûⁿli'eskâ'ï da'gûnstanehû'ⁿï ü`taâ'ta. Hiä`-nu:' nû'ⁿwâtï: Yâ'na-Unatsësdâ'gï tsana'sehâ'ï sâ'i-`nû Kâ'ga-Asgû'ⁿtagë tsana'sehâ'ï, sâi-`nû *Egû'ⁿli*-gwû, sâi-nû' (U)wa'sgilï tsïgï' Egû'ⁿlï Usdi'a tsïgï', nûⁿyâ'hi-`nû tsuyë`dâ'ï Yâ'na-Utsësdâgï naskiyû' tsïgï', usdi'-gwû tsïgï'. Egû'ⁿlï (u)wa'sgilï tsïgï'; sâ'ï Wâ'tige Unas(te')tsa tsïgï', sâ'i-`nû Û'ⁿage Tsunaste'tsa, Niga'ta unaste'tsa gesâ'ï.

Sunale'-gwû ale'ndï adanû'ⁿwâtï; tä'line e'ladï tsitkala'ï; tsâ'ine u'lsaladï'`satû'; nû'`kine igû' ts'kalâ'ï. Yeli'gwû' igesâ'ï. Nû'lstâiyanû'na gesâ'ï akanûⁿwi'skï, nasgwû' nulstaiyanû'na.

Translation.

FORMULA FOR TREATING THE CRIPPLER (RHEUMATISM).

Listen! Ha! In the Sun Land you repose, O Red Dog, O now you have swiftly drawn near to hearken. O great ada'wëhï[1] , you never fail in anything. O, appear and draw near running, for your prey never escapes. You are now come to remove the intruder. Ha! You have settled a very small part of it far off there at the end of the earth.

Listen! Ha! In the Frigid Land you repose, O Blue Dog. O now you have swiftly drawn near to hearken. O great ad'âw hï, you never fail in anything. O, appear and draw near running, for your prey never escapes. You are now come to remove the intruder. Ha! You have settled a very small part of it far off there at the end of the earth.

Listen! Ha! In the darkening land you repose, O Black Dog. O, now you have swiftly drawn near to hearken. O great ada'wëhi, you never fail in anything. O, appear and draw near running, for your prey never escapes. You are now come to remove the intruder. Ha! You have settled a very small part of it far off there at the end of the earth.

[1] *Ada'wëhï* is a word used to designate one supposed to have supernatural powers, and is applied alike to human beings and to the spirits invoked in the formulas. Some of the mythic heroes famous for their magic deeds are spoken of as *ada'wëhï* (plural *anida'wëhï* or *anida'we*), but in its application to mortals the term is used only of the very greatest shamans. None of those now belonging to the band are considered worthy of being thus called, although the term was sometimes applied to one, Usawï, who died some years ago. In speaking of himself as an ada'wëhï, as occurs in some of the formulas, the shaman arrogates to himself the same powers that belong to the gods. Our nearest equivalent is the word magician, but this falls far short of the idea conveyed by the Cherokee word. In the bible translation the word is used as the equivalent of angel or spirit

Listen! On Wa'halä you repose, O White Dog. Oh, now you have swiftly drawn near to hearken. O great ada'wëhï, you never fail in anything. Oh, appear and draw near running, for your prey never escapes. You are now come to remove the intruder. Ha! You have settled a very small part of it far off there at the end of the earth.

Listen! On Wa'halä, you repose, O White Terrapin. O, now you have swiftly drawn near to hearken. O great ada'wëhï, you never fail in anything. Ha! It is for you to loosen its hold on the bone. Relief is accomplished.

(Prescription.)--Lay a terrapin shell upon (the spot) and keep it there while the five kinds (of spirits) listen. On finishing, then blow once. Repeat four times, beginning each time from the start. On finishing the fourth time, then blow four times. Have two white beads lying in the shell, together with a little of the medicine. Don't interfere with it, but have a good deal boiling in another vessel--a bowl will do very well-- and rub it on warm while treating by applying the hands. And this is the medicine: What is called Yâ'na-Utsë'sta ("bear's bed," the Aspidium acrostichoides or Christmas fern); and the other is called Kâ'ga-Asgû'ⁿtagï ("crow's shin," the Adianthum pedatum or Maidenhair fern); and the other is the common Egû'ⁿlï (another fern); and the other is the Little Soft (-leaved) Egû'ⁿlï (Osmunda Cinnamonea or cinnamon fern), which grows in the rocks and resembles Yâna-Utsë'sta and is a small and soft (-leaved) Egû'ⁿlï. Another has brown roots and another has black roots. The roots of all should be (used).

Begin doctoring early in the morning; let the second (application) be while the sun is still near the horizon; the third when it has risen to a considerable height (10 a. m.); the fourth when it is above at noon. This is sufficient. (The doctor) must not eat, and the patient also must be fasting.

Explanation.

As this formula is taken from the manuscript of Gahuni, who died nearly thirty years ago, no definite statement of the theory of the disease, or its treatment, can be given, beyond what is contained in the formula itself, which, fortunately, is particularly explicit; most doctors contenting themselves with giving only the words of the prayer, without noting the ceremonies or even the medicine used. There are various theories as to the cause of each disease, the most common idea in regard to rheumatism being that it is caused by the spirits of. the slain animals, generally the deer, thirsting for vengeance on the hunter, as has been already explained in the myth of the origin of disease and medicine.

The measuring-worm (Catharis) is also held to cause rheumatism, from the resemblance of its motions to those of a rheumatic patient, and the name of the worm *wahïlï'* is frequently applied also to the disease.

There are formulas to propitiate the slain animals, but these are a part of the hunting code and can only be noticed here, although it may be mentioned in passing that the hunter, when about to return to the settlement, builds a fire in the path behind him, in order that the deer chief may not be able to follow him to his home. The disease, figuratively called the intruder (ulsgéta), is regarded as a living being, and the verbs used in speaking of it show that it is considered to be long, like a snake or fish. It is brought by the deer chief and put into the body, generally the limbs, of the hunter, who at once begins to suffer intense pain. It can be driven out only by some more powerful animal spirit which is the natural enemy of the deer, usually the dog or the wolf. These animal gods live up above beyond the seventh heaven and are the great prototypes of which the earthly animals are only diminutive copies. They are commonly located at the four cardinal points, each of which has a peculiar formulistic name and a special color which applies to everything in the same connection. Thus the east, north, west, and south are respectively the Sun Land, the Frigid Land, the Darkening Land, and Wä'halä', while their respective mythologic colors are Red, Blue, Black, and White. Wä'halä' is said to be a mountain far to the south. The white or red spirits are generally invoked for peace, health, and other blessings, the red alone for the success of an under taking, the blue spirits to defeat the schemes of an enemy or bring down troubles upon him, and the black to compass his death. The white and red spirits are regarded as the most powerful, and one of these two is generally called upon to accomplish the final result.

In this case the doctor first invokes the Red Dog in the Sun Land, calling him a great adáwehi, to whom nothing is impossible and who never fails to accomplish his purpose. He is addressed as if out of sight in the distance and is implored to appear running swiftly to the help of the sick man. Then the supplication changes to an assertion and the doctor declares that the Red Dog has already arrived to take the disease and has borne away a small portion of it to the uttermost ends of the earth. In the second, third, and fourth paragraphs the Blue Dog of the Frigid Land, the Black Dog of the Darkening Land, and the White Dog of Wä'halä' are successively invoked in the same terms and each bears away a portion of the disease and disposes of it in the same way. Finally, in the fifth paragraph, the White Terrapin of Wä'halä' is invoked. He bears off the remainder of the disease and the doctor declares that relief is accomplished. The connection of the terrapin in this formula is not evident, beyond the fact that he is regarded as having great influence in disease, and in this case the beads and a portion of the medicine are kept in a terrapin shell placed upon the diseased part while the prayer is being recited.

The formulas generally consist of four paragraphs, corresponding to four steps in the medical ceremony. In this case there are five, the last being addressed to the terrapin instead of to a dog. The prayers are recited in an undertone hardly audible at the distance of a few feet, with the exception of the frequent ha, which seems to be used as an interjection to attract attention and is always uttered in a louder tone. The beads--which are here white, symbolic of relief--are of common use in connection with these formulas, and are held between the thumb and finger, placed upon a cloth on the ground, or, as in this case, put into a terrapin shell along with a small portion of the medicine. According to directions, the shell has no other part in the ceremony.

The blowing is also a regular part of the treatment, the doctor either holding the medicine in his mouth and blowing it upon the patient, or, as it seems to be the case here, applying the medicine by rubbing, and blowing his breath upon the spot afterwards. In some formulas the simple blowing of the breath constitutes the whole application. In this instance the doctor probably rubs the medicine upon the affected part while reciting the first paragraph in a whisper, after which he blows once upon the spot. The other paragraphs are recited in the same manner, blowing once after each. In this way the whole formula is repeated four times, with four blows at the end of the final repetition. The directions imply that the doctor blows only at the end of the whole formula, but this is not in accord with the regular mode of procedure and seems to be a mistake.

The medicine consists of a warm decoction of the roots of four varieties of fern, rubbed on with the hand. The awkward description of the species shows how limited is the Indian's power of botanic classification. The application is repeated four times during the same morning, beginning just at daybreak and ending at noon. Four is the sacred number running through every detail of these formulas, there being commonly four spirits invoked in four paragraphs, four blowings with four final blows, four herbs in the decoction, four applications, and frequently four days' gaktu^n'ta or tabu. In this case no tabu is specified beyond the fact that both doctor and patient must be fasting. The tabu generally extends to salt or lye, hot food and women, while in rheumatism some doctors forbid the patient to eat the foot or leg of any animal, the reason given being that the limbs are generally the seat of the disease. For a similar reason the patient is also forbidden to eat or even to touch a squirrel, a buffalo, a eat, or any animal which "humps" itself. In the same way a scrofulous patient must not eat turkey, as that bird seems to have a scrofulous eruption on its head, while ball players must abstain from eating frogs, because the bones of that animal are brittle and easily broken.

AND THIS ALSO IS FOR TREATING THE CRIPPLER

HIÄ-NÛ' NASGWÛ' DIDÛ^{n}LË'SKÏ ADÂNÛ'^{n}WÂTÏ.

Asga'ya yûkanû'^{n}wï
Agë`ya Giagage'ï atätï';
agë'`ya-nû yûkanû'^{n}wï
Asga'ya Gigage'ï atätï'.

Yû! Higë'`ya Gigage'ï tsûdante'lûhï gese'ï. Ulsge'ta hi'tsanu'y`tani'leï. Ha-Nû^{n}dâgû'^{n}yï nû^{n}ta'tsûdälenû'hï gese'ï. Gasgilâ' gigage'ï tsusdi'ga tetsadï'ilë' detsala'siditë-gë'ï. Hanâ'gwa usïnuli'yu detsaldisi'yûï.

Utsï(nä')wa nu'tatanû'^{n}ta. Usû'hita nutanû'na. Utsïnä'wa-gwû nigû^{n}tisge'stï.

(Degâ'sisisgû'^{n}ï)--Hiä-gwû' nigaû' kanâhe'ta. Nû'`kiha nagû'n-kw?tisgâ' dagû'$^n$stiskû'ï. Sâ'gwa nû$^n$skwiû'ta gûnstû'$^n$ï agûnstagi's-kâï hû$^n$tsatasgâ'ï nû'`kine-`nû û$^n$skwû'ta nû'`kï nû^{n}tsâtasgâ'ï. Hiâ`nû' nû$^n$wâtï: Egû'$^n$lï, Yâ'na-`nû Utsësdâ'gï, (U)wa'sgilï tsïgï' Egû'^{n}lï, tä'lï tsinu'dalë'ha, Kâ'ga-`nû Asgû'$^n$tagë tsiû$^n$nâ'sehâ'ï, Da'yï-`nû Uwâ'yï tsiû^{n}nâ'sehâ'ï. Su'talï iyutale'gï unaste'tsa agâ'tï, uga'nawû-`nû' dagûnsta'`tisgâ'ï nû'^{n}wâtî asû^{n}ga`la'ï. Usû'hï adanû'$^n$wâtï. nu'`kï tsusû'hita dulsi'nisû'^{n} adanû'^{n}wâtï. Ä`nawa'gi-`nû dilasula'gï gesû'^{n}ï ûlë' tsïkani'kaga'ï gûw`sdi'-gwû utsawa'ta ä`nawa'-gwû-nû'.

Hiä-nû' gaktû'^{n}ta gûlkwâ'gï tsusû'hita. Gû'^{n}wädana'datlahistï' nige'sû^{n}na--Salâ'lï, gi`li-`nû, wë'sa-'nû, ä'tatsû-nû', a'mä-'nû', ani-gë'`ya-nû. Uda`lï' ya'kanû^{n}wi'ya nû'`kiha tsusû'hita unädanä'lâtsi-tustï nige'sû$^n$na. Gasgilâ'gi-`nû uwä'su^n-gwû u'skïladi'stï uwä'sû nû'`kï tsusû'hitä'. Disâ'i-`nû dega'sgilâ û'^{n}tsa nû`nä' uwa'`tï yigesûï nû'`kï tsusû'hita.

Translation.

AND THIS ALSO IS FOR TREATING THE CRIPPLER.

Yû! O Red Woman, you have caused it. You have put the intruder under him. Ha! now you have come from the Sun Land. You have brought the small red seats, with your feet resting upon them. Ha! now they have swiftly moved away from you. Relief is accomplished. Let it not be for one night alone. Let the relief come at once.

(Prescription)--(*corner note at top.*) If treating a man one must say *Red Woman*, and if treating a woman one must say *Red Man*.

This is just all of the prayer. Repeat it four times while laying on the hands. After saying it over once, with the hands on (the body of the patient), take off the hands and blow once, and at the fourth repetition blow four times. And this is the medicine. Egû'ⁿlï (a species of fern). Yâ'-na-Utsë'sta ("bear's bed," the Aspidium acrostichoides or Christmas fern), *two* varieties of the soft-(leaved) Egû'ⁿlï (one, the small variety, is the Cinnamon fern, Osmunda cinnamonea), and what is called Kâ'ga Asgû'ⁿtagë ("crow's shin," the Adiantum pedatum or Maidenhair fern) and what is called Da'yï-Uwâ'yï ("beaver's paw"--not identified). Boil the roots of the six varieties together and apply the hands warm with the medicine upon them. Doctor in the evening. Doctor four consecutive nights. (The pay) is cloth and moccasins; or, if one does not have them, just a little dressed deerskin and some cloth.

And this is the tabu for seven nights. One must not touch a squirrel, a dog, a cat, the mountain trout, or women. If one is treating a married man they (sic) must not touch his wife for four nights. And he must sit on a seat by himself for four nights, and must not sit on the other seats for four nights.

Explanation.

The treatment and medicine in this formula are nearly the same as in that just given, which is also for rheumatism, both being written by Gahuni. The prayer differs in several respects from any other obtained, but as the doctor has been dead for years it is impossible to give a full explanation of all the points. This is probably the only formula in the collection in which the spirit invoked is the "Red Woman," but, as explained in the corner note at the top, this is only the form used instead of "Red Man," when the patient is a man. The Red Man, who is considered perhaps the most powerful god in the Cherokee pantheon, is in some way connected with the thunder, and is invoked in a large number of formulas. The change in the formula, according to the sex of the patient, brings to mind a belief in Irish folk medicine, that in applying certain remedies the doctor and patient must be of opposite sexes. The Red Man lives in the east, in accordance with the regular mythologic color theory, as already explained. The seats also are red, and the form of the verb indicates that the Red Woman is either standing upon them (plural) or sitting with her feet resting upon the rounds. These seats or chairs are frequently mentioned in the formulas, and always correspond in color with the spirit invoked. It is not clear why the Red Woman is held responsible for the disease, which is generally attributed to the revengeful efforts of the game, as already explained. In agreement with the regular form, the disease is said to be put under (not into) the patient. The assertion that the chairs "have swiftly moved away" would seem from analogy to mean that the disease has been placed upon the seats and thus borne away. The verb implies that the seats move by their own volition. Immediately afterward it is declared that relief is accomplished. The expression "usû'hita nutanû'na" occurs frequently in these formulas, and may mean either "let it not be for one night alone," or "let it not stay a single night," according to the context.

The directions specify not only the medicine and the treatment, but also the doctor's fee. From the form of the verb the tabu, except as regards the seat to be used by the sick person, seems to apply to both doctor and patient. It is not evident why the mountain trout is prohibited, but the dog, squirrel, and cat are tabued, as already explained, from the fact that these animals frequently assume positions resembling the cramped attitude common to persons afflicted by rheumatism. The cat is considered especially uncanny, as coming from the whites. Seven, as well as four, is a sacred number with the tribe, being also the number of their gentes. It will be noted that time is counted by nights instead of by days.

THIS IS TO TREAT THEM IF THEY ARE BITTEN BY A SNAKE

HIÂ' I'NATÛ YUNISKÛ'LTSA ADANÛ'NWÂTÎ.

1. *Dûnu'wa*, dûnu'wa, dûnu'wa, dûnu'wa, dûnu'wa, dûnu'wa (*song*).
    Sgë! Ha-Walâ'sï-gwû tsûⁿlû'ⁿtani'ga.
2. Dayuha, dayuha, dayuha, dayuha dayuha (*song*).
    Sgë! Ha-*Usugï*-gwû tsûⁿ-lûⁿ'-tani'ga.

(Degâ'sisisgû'ⁿï).--Kanâgi'ta nâyâ'ga hiä' dilentisg'ûⁿï. Ta'lï igû'n-kw?ta`tï, ûlë' talinë' tsutanû'ⁿna nasgwû' tâ'lï igû'nkw?ta`tï. Tsâ'la aganû'ⁿlieskâï' tsâ'la yikani'gûⁿgû'âï' watsi'la-gwû ganûⁿli'yëtï uniskûl`tsû'ⁿï. Nû'`kï nagade'stisgâï' aganûⁿli'esgûⁿï. Akskû'nï gades-t'a`tï, nûû`kï nagade' sta hûⁿtsatasgâ'ï. Hiä-`nû' i'natû akti'sï udestâ'ï yigû'n`ka, naski-`nû' tsagadû'lägisgâ'ï iyu'stï gatgû'ⁿi.

Translation.

THIS IS TO TREAT THEM IF THEY ARE BITTEN BY A SNAKE.

1. Dûnu'wa, dûnu'wa, dûnu'wa, dûnu'wa, dûnu'wa, dûnu'wa.
   Listen! Ha! It is only a common frog which has passed by and put it (the intruder) into you.
2. Dayuha', dayuha, dayuha, dayuha, dayuha.
   Listen! Ha! It is only an *Us'`gï* which has passed by and put it into you.

(Prescription.)--Now this at the beginning is a song. One should say it twice and also say the second line twice. Rub tobacco (juice) on the bite for some time, or if there be no tobacco just rub on saliva once. In rubbing it on, one must go around four times. Go around toward the left and blow four times in a circle. This is because in lying down the snake always coils to the right and this is just the same (*lit.* "means like") as uncoiling it.

Explanation.

This is also from the manuscript book of Gahuni, deceased, so that no explanation could be obtained from the writer. The formula consists of a song of two verses, each followed by a short recitation.

The whole is repeated, according to the directions, so as to make four verses or songs; four, as already stated, being the sacred number running through most of these formulas. Four blowings and four circuits in the rubbing are also specified. The words used in the songs are sometimes composed of unmeaning syllables, but in this case dûnuwa and dayuha seem to have a meaning, although neither the interpreter nor the shaman consulted could explain them, which may be because the words have become altered in the song, as frequently happens. Dûnu'wa appears to be an old verb, meaning "it has penetrated," probably referring to the tooth of the reptile. These medicine songs are always sung in a low plaintive tone, somewhat resembling a lullaby. Usu'`gï also is without explanation, but is probably the name of some small reptile or batrachian.

As in this case the cause of the trouble is evident, the Indians have no theory to account for it. It may be remarked, however, that when one dreams of being bitten, the same treatment and ceremonies must be used as for the actual bite; otherwise, although perhaps years afterward, a similar inflammation will appear on the spot indicated in the dream, and will be followed by the same fatal consequences, The rattlesnake is regarded as a supernatural being or ada'wehi, whose favor must be propitiated, and great pains are taken not to offend him. In consonance with this idea it is never said among the people that a person has been bitten by a snake, but that he has been "scratched by a brier." In the same way, when an eagle has been shot for a ceremonial dance, it is announced that "a snowbird has been killed," the purpose being to deceive the rattlesnake or eagle spirits which might be listening.

The assertion that it is "only a common frog" or" only an Usu'?gï brings out another characteristic idea of these formulas. Whenever the ailment is of a serious character, or, according to the Indian theory, whenever it is due to the influence of some powerful disease spirit the doctor always endeavors to throw contempt upon the intruder, and convince it of his own superior power by asserting the sickness to be the work of some inferior being, just as a white physician might encourage a patient far gone with consumption by telling him that the, illness was only a slight cold. Sometimes there is a regular scale of depreciation, the doctor first ascribing the disease to a rabbit or groundhog or some other weak animal, then in succeeding paragraphs mentioning other still less important animals and finally declaring it to be the work of a mouse, a small fish, or some other insignificant creature. In this instance an ailment caused by the rattlesnake, the most dreaded of the animal spirits, is ascribed to a frog, one of the least importance.

In applying the remedy the song is probably sung while rubbing the tobacco juice around the wound. Then the short recitation is repeated and the doctor blows four times in a circle about the spot.

The whole ceremony is repeated four times. The curious directions for uncoiling the snake have parallels in European folk medicine.

TO TREAT THEM WHEN SOMETHING IS CAUSING SOMETHING TO EAT THEM

GÛⁿWÂNI'GISTÂ'Ï ADANU'ⁿWÂTÏ.

Sgë! Ha-tsida'wëiyu, gahus'tï aginúl`tï nige'sûⁿna. Gûⁿgwäda-g'anad?diyû' tsida'wëi'yu. Ha-Wähuhu'-gwû hitagu'sgastanë`hëï. Ha-nâ'gwa hü`kikahûⁿnû' ha-dustü`'gahï digesû'ⁿï, iyû'ⁿta wûⁿ`kidâ'-hïstani'ga.

Sgë! Ha-tsida'wëi'yu, gahu'stï aginu'l`tï nige'sûⁿna. Gûⁿgwä-daga'nad?diyû' tsida'wëi'yu. Ha-Uguku'-gwû hitagu'sgastanë'hëï udâhi'yu tag'u'sgastanë'hëï. Ha-na'gwadi'na hûⁿkikahûⁿnû'. Hanânâ'hï digesû'ⁿï, iyû'ⁿta wûⁿ`kidâ'hïstani'ga.

Sgë! Ha-tsida'wëi'yu, gahu'stï aginu'l`tï nige'sûⁿna. Gûⁿgwäda-ga'nad?diyû tsida'wëi'yu. Ha-Tsistu-gwû hitagu'sgastanë'hë'ï udâhi'yu tagu'sgastanë'hëï. Ha-nâ'gwadi'na hû'ⁿkikahû'ⁿnû. Ha-sunûⁿda'sï iyû'ⁿta kane'skawâ'dihï digesû'ⁿï, wûⁿ`kidâ'hïstani'ga.

Sgë! Ha-tsida'wëi'yu, gahu'stï aginu'l`tï nige'sûⁿna. Gûⁿgwädaga'nad?di'yû tsida'wëi'yu. Ha-De'tsata'-gwû (hi)tagu'sgastanë'hëï udâhi'yu tagu'sgastanë'hëï. Ha-nâ'gwadi'na hûⁿkikahû'ⁿna. Ha-udâ'tale'ta digesû'ⁿï, iyû'ⁿta wûⁿ`kidâ'hïstani'ga.

(Degâ'sisisgû'ⁿï)-Hiä'-skïnï' unsdi'ya dïkanû'ⁿwâtï tsa`natsa'yihâ'ï tsaniska'iha'ï; gûⁿwani'gista'ï hi'anûdï'sgaï'. Ämä' dûtsati'stïsgâ'ï nû`'kï tsusû'hita dïkanû'ⁿwâtï Ulsinide'na dakanû'ⁿwisgâ'ï. Û'ⁿtsa iyû'ⁿta witunini'dastï yigesâ'ï.

Translation.

TO TREAT THEM WHEN SOMETHING IS CAUSING SOMETHING TO EAT THEM.

Listen! Ha! I am a great ada'wehi, I never fail in anything. I surpass all others-I am a great ada'wehi. Ha! It is a mere screech owl that has frightened him. Ha! now I have put it away in the laurel thickets. There I compel it to remain,

Listen! Ha! I am a great ada'wehi, I never fail in anything. I surpass all others--I am a great ada'wehi. Ha! It is a mere hooting owl that has frightened him. Undoubtedly that has frightened him. Ha! At once I have put it away in the spruce thickets. Ha! There I compel it to remain.

Listen! Ha! I am a great ada'wehi, I never fail in anything. I surpass all others--I am a great ada'wehi. Ha! It is only a rabbit that has frightened him. Undoubtedly that has frightened him. Ha! Instantly I have put it away on the mountain ridge. Ha! There in the broom sage I compel it to remain.

Listen! Ha! I am a great ada'wehi, I never fail in anything. I surpass all others--I am a great ada'wehi. Ha! It is only a mountain sprite that has frightened him. Undoubtedly that has frightened him. Ha! Instantly I have put it away on the bluff. Ha! There I compel it to remain.

(Prescription)--Now this is to treat infants if they are affected by crying and nervous fright. (Then) it is said that something is causing something to eat them. To treat them one may blow water on them for four nights. Doctor them just before dark. Be sure not to carry them about outside the house.

Explanation.

The Cherokee name for this disease is Gu^{n}wani'gistâï', which signifies that "something is causing something to eat," or gnaw the vitals of the patient. The disease attacks only infants of tender age and the symptoms are nervousness and troubled sleep, from which the child wakes suddenly crying as if frightened. The civilized doctor would regard these as symptoms of the presence of worms, but although the Cherokee name might seem to indicate the same belief, the real theory is very different.

Cherokee mothers sometimes hush crying children by telling them that the screech owl is listening out in the woods or that the De'tsata-- a malicious little dwarf who lives in caves in the river bluffs--will come and get them. This quiets the child for the time and is so far successful, but the animals, or the De'tsata, take offense at being spoken of in this way, and visit their displeasure upon the *children born to the mother afterward*. This they do by sending an animal into the body of the child to gnaw its vitals. The disease is very common and there are several specialists who devote their attention to it, using various formulas and prescriptions. It is also called ätawi'nëhï, signifying that it is caused by the "dwellers in the forest," i. e., the wild game and birds, and some doctors declare that it is caused by the revengeful comrades of the animals, especially birds, killed by the father of the child, the animals tracking the slayer to his home by the blood drops on the leaves. The next formula will throw more light upon this theory.

In this formula the doctor, who is certainly not overburdened with modesty, starts out by asserting that he is a great ada'wehi, who never fails and who surpasses all others. He then declares that, the disease is caused by a more screech owl, which he at once banishes to the laurel thicket. In the succeeding paragraphs he reiterates his former boasting, but asserts in turn that the trouble is caused by a mere hooting owl, a rabbit, or even by the De'tsata, whose greatest exploit is hiding the arrows of the boys, for which the youthful hunters do not hesitate to rate him soundly. These various mischief-makers the doctor banishes to their proper haunts, the hooting owl to the spruce thicket, the rabbit to the broom sage. on the mountain side, and the, De'tsata to the bluffs along the river bank.

Some doctors use herb decoctions, which are blown upon the body of the child, but in this formula the only remedy prescribed is water, which must be blown upon the body of the little sufferer just before dark for four nights. The regular method is to blow once each at the end of the first, second, and third paragraphs and four times at the end of the fourth or last. In diseases of this kind, which are not supposed to be of a local character, the doctor blows first upon the back of the head, then upon the left shoulder, next upon the right shoulder, and finally upon the breast, the patient being generally sitting, or propped up in bed, facing the east. The child must not be taken out of doors during the four days, because should a bird chance to fly overhead so that its shadow would fall upon the infant, it would *fan the disease* back into the body of the little one.

TO TREAT GÛⁿWANI'GISTÛ'ⁿÏ--(SECOND).

GÛⁿWANI'GISTÛ'ⁿÏ DITANÛⁿWÂTI'YÏ.

Yû! Sgë! Usïnu'lï hatû'ⁿgani'ga, Giya'giya' Sa`ka'nï, ew?satâ'gï tsûl`dâ'histï. Usïnu'lï hatlasi'ga. Tsis'kwa-gwû' ulsge'ta uwu'tlani`lëï'. Usïnuli'yu atsahilu'gïsi'ga. Utsïnä'wa nu'tatanû'ⁿta. Yü!

Yû! Sgë! Usïnu'lï hatûⁿgani'ga, Diga'tiskï Wâtige'ï, galû'ⁿlatï iyû'ⁿta ditsûl`dâ'histï. Ha-nâ'gwa usïnu'lï hatlasi'ga. Tsi'skwa-gwû dïtu'nila'- w?itsû'hï higese'ï. Usïnûlï kë'`tati'gû`lahi'ga. Utsïnä'wa adûⁿni'ga. Yû!

Translation.

TO TREAT GÛⁿWANI'GISTÛ'ⁿÏ--(SECOND).

Yû! Listen! Quickly you have drawn near to hearken, O Blue Sparrow-Hawk; in the spreading tree tops you are at rest. Quickly you have come down. The intruder is only a bird which has, overshadowed him. Swiftly you have swooped down upon it. Relief is accomplished. Yû!

Yû! Listen! Quickly you have drawn near to hearken, O Brown Rabbit-Hawk; you are at rest there above. Ha! Swiftly now you have come down. It is only the birds which have come together for a council. Quickly you have come and scattered them. Relief is accomplished. Yû!

Explanation.

This formula, also for Gûⁿwani'gistû'ⁿï or Atawinë'hï, was obtained from A`wan'ita (Young Deer), who wrote down only the prayer and explained the treatment orally. He coincides in the opinion that this disease in children is caused by the birds, but says that it originates from the shadow of a bird. flying overhead having fallen upon the pregnant mother. He says further that the disease is easily recognized in children, but that it sometimes does not develop until the child has attained maturity, when it is more difficult to discern the cause of the trouble, although in the latter case dark circles around the eyes are unfailing symptoms.

The prayer--like several others from the same source--seems incomplete, and judging from analogy is evidently incorrect in some respects, but yet exemplifies the disease theory in a striking manner. The disease is declared to have been caused by the birds, it being asserted in the first paragraph that a bird has cast its shadow upon the sufferer, while in the second it is declared that they have gathered in council (in his body). This latter is a favorite expression in these formulas to indicate the great number of the disease animals.

Another expression of frequent occurrence is to the effect that the disease animals have formed a settlement or established a townhouse in the patient's body. The disease animal, being a bird or birds, must be dislodged by something which preys upon birds, and accordingly the Blue Sparrow-Hawk from the tree tops and the Brown Rabbit-Hawk (Diga'tiskï--"One who snatches up"), from above are invoked to drive out the intruders. The former is then said to have swooped down upon them as a hawk darts upon its prey, while the latter is declared to have scattered the birds which were holding a council. This being done, relief is accomplished. Yû! is a meaningless interjection frequently used to introduce or close paragraphs or songs.

The medicine used is a warm decoction of the bark of Kûnstû'tsï (Sassafras--Sassafras officinale), Kanû^{n}si'ta (Flowering Dogwood--Cornus florida), Udâ'lana (Service tree--Amelanchier Canadensis), and Uni'kwa (Black Gum--Nyssa multiflora), with the roots of two species (large and small) of Da'yakalï'skï (Wild Rose--Rosa lucida). The bark in every case is taken from the east side of the tree, and the roots selected are also generally, if not always, those growing toward the east. In this case the roots and barks are not bruised, but are simply steeped in warm water for four days. The child is then stripped and bathed all over with the decoction morning and night for four days, no formula being used during the bathing. It is then made to hold up its hands in front of its face with the palms turned out toward the doctor, who takes some of the medicine in his mouth and repeats the prayer mentally, blowing the medicine upon the head and hands of the patient at the, final *Yû!* of each paragraph. It is probable that the prayer originally consisted of four paragraphs, or else that these two paragraphs were repeated. The child drinks a little of the medicine at the end of each treatment.

The use of salt is prohibited during the four days of the treatment, the word (amä') being understood to include lye, which enters largely into Cherokee food preparations. No chicken or other feathered animal is allowed to enter the house during the same period, for obvious reasons, and strangers are excluded for reasons already explained.

THIS TELLS ABOUT MOVING PAINS IN THE TEETH (NEURALGIA?).

HIA' DU'NIYUKWATISGÛⁿÎ KANA'HÈHÛ.

Sgë! Nûⁿdâgûⁿyï tsûl`dâ'histï, Kanani'ski Gigage. Usïnu'lï nûⁿnâ gi'gage hïnûⁿni'ga. Hida'wëhi-gâgû', astï' digi'gage usïnû'lï dehïkssa'ûⁿtani'ga. Ulsge'ta kane'ge kayu'`ga gesû'ⁿ, tsgâ'ya-gwû higese'ï. Ehïstï' hituwa'saniy?teï'. Usïnu'lï astï' digi'gage dehada'ûⁿtani'ga, adi'na tsûlstai-yû'`ti-gwû higese'ï. Nâ'gwa gânagi'ta da'tsatane'lï. Utsïnä'wa nu'tatanû'ⁿta nûⁿtûneli'ga. Yû!

Hïgayû'ⁿlï Tsûne'ga hatû'ⁿgani'ga. "A'ya-gâgû' gatû'ⁿgisge'stï tsûngili'sï deagwûlstawï'stitege'stï," tsadûnû'hï. Na'ski-gâgû' itsa'-wesû'hï nâ'gwa usïnu'lï hatû'ⁿgani'ga. Utsïnä'wa nútatanû'ta nûⁿtû'neli'ga. Yû!

Sgë! Uhyûⁿtlâ'yï tsûl`dâ'histi Kanani'skï Sa`ka'nï. Usïnu'lï nûⁿnâ sa`ka'nï hïnûⁿni'ga. Hida'wëhi-gâgû', astï' (di)sa'ka'nï usïnu'lï dehïksa'ûⁿtani'ga. Ulsge'ta kane'ge kayu'`ga gesû'ⁿ, tsgâ'ya-gwû higese'ï. Ehïstï' hituwa'saniy?te(ï'). Usïnu'lï astï' disa`ka'nige dehada'ûⁿtaniga, adi'na tsûlstai-yû'`ti-gwû higese'ï. Nâ'gwa tsgâ'ya gûnagi'ta tsûtûneli'ga. Utsïnä'wa nu'tatanû'ⁿta nûⁿtûneli'ga. Yû!

Hïgayû'ⁿlï Tsûne'ga hatûⁿgani'ga. "A'ya-gâgû' gatû'ⁿgisge'stï tsûngili'sï deagwûlstawï'stitege'stï," tsadûnû'hï. Nas'kigâgû' itsawesû'hï nâ'gwa usïnu'lï hatû'ⁿgani'ga. Utsïnä'wa nutatanû'ⁿta nûⁿtûneli'ga. Yû!

Sgë! Usûhi'yï tsûl`dâ'histï Kanani'skï Û'ⁿnage. Usïnu'lï nûⁿnâ û'ⁿnage hïnûⁿni'ga. Hida'wëhi-gâgû', astï' digû'ⁿnage usïnu'lï dehïksa'ûⁿtani'ga. Ulsge'ta kane'ge kayu'`ga gesû'ⁿ, tsâgâ'ya-gwû higese'ï. Ehïstï' hituwa'saniy`teï'. Usïnu'lï astï' digû'ⁿnage dehada'ûⁿtani'ga, adi'na tsûlstai-yû'`ti-gwû higese'ï. Nâ'gwa tsgâ'ya gûnagi'ta tsûtûneli'ga. Utsïnä'wa nutatanû'ⁿta nûⁿtûneli'ga. Yû!

Hïgayû'ⁿlï Tsûne'ga hatûⁿgani'ga. "A'ya-gâgû' gatû'ⁿgisge'stï tsûngili'sï deagwûlstawï'stitege'stï," tsadûnû'hï. Na'skigâgû' itsawesû'hï nâ'gwa usïnu'li hatû'ⁿgani'ga. Utsïnä'wa nutatanû'ⁿta nûⁿtûneli'ga. Yû!

Sgë! Galû'ⁿlatï tsûl`dâ'histï, Kanani'skï Tsûne'ga. Usïnu'lï nûⁿnâ une'ga hïnûⁿni'ga. Hida'wëhi-gâgû', astï' tsune'ga usïnu'lï dehïksa'ûⁿ tani'ga.

Ulsge'ta kane'ge kayu'ʿga gesû'ⁿ, tsgâ'ya-gwû higese'ï. Ehïstï' hituwa'säniy`teï'. Usïnu'lï astï' tsune'ga dehada'ûⁿtani'ga, adi'na tsûlstai-yû'ʿti-gwû higese'ï. Nâ'gwa tsgâ'ya gûnagi'ta tsûtûneli'ga. Utsïnä'wa nu'tatanû'ⁿta, nûⁿtûneli'ga. Yû!

Hïgayû'ⁿlï Tsûne'ga hatû'ⁿgani'ga. "A'ya-gâgû' gatû'ⁿgisge'stï tsûngili'sï deagwûlstawï'stitege'stï," tsadûnû'hï. Naski-gâgû' itsawesû'hï nâ'gwa usïnu'lï hatûⁿgani'ga. U'tsïnä'wa nutatanû'ⁿta nûⁿtûneli'ga. Yû!

(Degasi'sisgû'ⁿï)--Hiä' duniyukwa'tisgû'ⁿï dïkanû'ⁿwâtï ätanû'ⁿsida'hï yï'gï. Na'skï digû'nstanë'ʿti-gwû ûlë' tsïtsâtû' yie'lisû. Nigûⁿ'-gwû usû'na [for usûnda'na?] gû'ⁿtatï nayâ'ga nû'ⁿwatï unanû'ⁿskä`la'ï. Kane'ska dalâ'nige unaste'tla tsï'gï. Se'lu dïgahû`nû'hï tsuni'yahïstï' nû'ʿkï tsusû'hita, kanâhe'na-`nû naskï' iga'ï udanû'stï hi'gï nayâ'ga.

Translation.

THIS TELLS ABOUT MOVING PAINS IN THE TEETH (NEURALGIA?).

Listen! In the Sunland you repose, O Red Spider. Quickly you have brought and laid down the red path. O great ada'wehi, quickly you have brought down the red threads from above. The intruder in the tooth has spoken and it is only a worm. The tormentor has wrapped itself around the root of the tooth. Quickly you have dropped down the red threads, for it is just what you eat. Now it is for you to pick it up. The relief has been caused to come. Yû!

O Ancient White, you have drawn near to hearken, for you have said, "When I shall hear my grandchildren, I shall hold up their heads." Because you have said it, now therefore you have drawn near to listen. The relief has been caused to come. Yû!

Listen! In the Frigid Land you repose, O Blue Spider. Quickly you have brought and laid down the blue path. O great ada'wehi, quickly you have brought down the blue threads from above. The intruder in the tooth has spoken and it is only a worm. The tormentor has wrapped itself around the root of the tooth. Quickly you have dropped down the blue threads, for it is just what you eat. Now it is for you to pick it up. The relief has been caused to come. Yû!

O Ancient White, you have drawn near to hearken, for you have said, "When I shall hear my grandchildren, I shall hold up their heads." Because you have said it, now therefore you have drawn near to listen. The relief has been caused to come. Yû!

Listen! In the Darkening Land you repose, O Black Spider. Quickly you have brought and laid down the black path. O great ada'wehi, quickly you have brought down the black threads from above. The intruder in the tooth has spoken and it is only a worm. The tormentor has wrapped itself around the root of the tooth. Quickly you have dropped down the black threads, for it is just what you eat. Now it is for you to pick it up. The relief has been caused to come. Yû!

O Ancient White, you have drawn near to hearken, for you have said, "When I shall hear my grandchildren, I shall hold up their heads." Because you have said it, now therefore you have drawn near to listen. The relief has been caused to come. Yû!

Listen! You repose on high, O White Spider. Quickly you have brought and laid down the white path. O great ada'wehi, quickly you have brought down the white threads from above. The intruder in the tooth has spoken and it is only a worm. The tormentor has wrapped itself around the root of the tooth. Quickly you have dropped down the white threads, for it is just what you eat. Now it is for you to pick it up. The relief has been caused to come. Yû!

O Ancient White, you have drawn near to hearken, for you have said, "When I shall hear my grandchildren, I shall hold up their heads." Because you have said it, now therefore you have drawn near to listen. The relief has been caused to come. Yû!

(Prescription)--This is to treat them if there are pains moving about in the teeth. It is only (necessary) to lay on the hands, or to blow, if one should prefer. One may use any kind of a tube, but usually they have the medicine in the mouth. It is the Yellow-rooted Grass (kane'ska dalâ'nige unaste'tla; not identified.) One must abstain four nights from cooked corn (hominy), and kanâhe'na (fermented corn gruel) is especially forbidden during the same period.

Explanation.

This formula is taken from the manuscript book of Gatigwanasti, now dead, and must therefore be explained from general analogy. The ailment is described as "pains moving about in the teeth"--that is, affecting several teeth simultaneously--and appears to be neuralgia. The disease spirit is called "the intruder" and "the tormentor" and is declared to be a mere worm (tsgâ'ya), which has wrapped itself around the base of the tooth. This is the regular toothache theory. The doctor then calls upon the Red Spider of the Sunland to let down the red threads from above, along the red path, and to take up the intruder, which is just what the spider eats. The same prayer is addressed in turn to the Blue Spider in the north, the Black Spider in the west and the White Spider above (galûⁿ'lati). It may be stated here that all these spirits are supposed to dwell above, but when no point of the compass is assigned, galûⁿ'lati is understood to mean directly overhead, but far above everything of earth. The dweller in this overhead galûⁿ'lati may be red, white, or brown in color. In this formula it is white, the ordinary color assigned spirits dwelling in the south. In another toothache formula the Squirrel is implored to take the worm and put it between the forking limbs of a tree on the north side of the mountain.

Following each supplication to the spider is another addressed to the Ancient White, the formulistic name for fire. The name refers to its antiquity and light-giving properties and perhaps also to the fact that when dead it is covered with a coat of white ashes. In those formulas in which the hunter draws omens from the live coals it is frequently addressed as the Ancient Red.

The directions are not explicit and must be interpreted from analogy. "Laying on the hands" refers to pressing the thumb against the jaw over the aching tooth, the hand having been previously warmed over the fire, this being a common method of treating toothache. The other method suggested is to blow upon the spot (tooth or outside of jaw?) a decoction of an herb described rather vaguely as "yellow-rooted grass" either through a tube or from the mouth of the operator. Igawï', a toothache specialist, treats this ailment either by pressure with the warm thumb, or by blowing tobacco smoke from a pipe placed directly against the tooth. Hominy and fermented corn gruel (kanâhe'na) are prohibited for the regular term of four nights, or, as we are accustomed to say, four days, and special emphasis is laid upon the gruel tabu.

The prayer to the Spider is probably repeated while the doctor is warming his hands over the fire, and the following paragraph to the Ancient White (the Fire) while holding the warm thumb upon the aching spot. This reverses the usual order, which is to address the fire while warming the hands. In this connection it must be noted that the fire used by the doctor is never the ordinary fire on the hearth, but comes from four burning chips taken from the hearth fire and generally placed in an earthen vessel by the side of the patient. In some cases the decoction is heated by putting into it seven live coals taken from the fire on the hearth.

TO TREAT THE GREAT CHILL

UNAWA STÎ EGWA (ADANÛⁿWATÏ).

Sgë! Galûⁿlatï' hinehi'(2) hinehi'yû(3) hinida'we(4), utsinâ'wa(5) adûⁿniga(6)

       1 2 1 2 2 2 3 4 3 3 5 6 6--Hayï'!

Sgë! Uⁿwadâ'hi(1) hinehi'(2), hinehi'yû(3) hinida'we(4) utsinâ'wa(5) adûⁿni'ga(6)

       1 2 1 2 2 2 3 4 3 3 5 6 6--Hayï'!

Sgë! Nâtsihi'(1) hinehi'(2) hinehi'yû(3) hinida'we(4) utsinâ'wa(5) adûⁿni'ga(6)

       1 2 1 2 2 2 3 4 3 3 5 6 6--Hayï'!

Sgë! Amâyi'(1) hinehi'(2), hinehi'yû(3) hinida'we(4) utsinâ'wa(5) adûⁿni'ga(6)

       1 2 1 2 2 2 3 3 3 3 5 6 6--Hayï'!

Sgë! Ha-nâ'gwa hatû'ⁿgani'ga, Agalu'ga Tsûsdi'ga, hida'wëhï, â'tali tsusdiga'hï duda'w?satû'ⁿ ditsûldâ'histï. (Hida'wëhï, gahu'stï tsanu'lûⁿhûⁿsgï' nige'sûⁿna.) Ha-nâ'gwa da'tûlehûⁿgû'. Usdi'gi(yu) utiya'stanûⁿ'(hï) (higese'i). (Hûⁿ)hiyala'gistani'ga igä'tï usdigâ'hï usa'hïlagï' Igâtu'ltï nûⁿnâ'hï wïte'tsatänûⁿ'ûⁿsï'.
A`ne'tsâge'ta *getsatûnëhï*nûⁿgûlstani'ga igûⁿ'wûlstanita'sti-gwû. Ati'gale'yata tsûtû'neli'ga. Utsïnâ'wa (¹) nigûⁿtisge'stï.

Sgë! Ha-nâ'gwa hûⁿhatû'ⁿgani'ga, Agalu'ga Hegwahigwû'. Â'talï tsegwâ'hï duda'w?satûⁿ iyûⁿta ditsûldâ'histï. Agalu'ga He'gwa, hausïnu'lï da'tûlehûⁿgû. Usdi'giyu utiya'stanûⁿhï. Hiyala'gistani'ga ulsge'ta igâ't-egwâ'hï) usa'hïlagï'. (Igat-(egwâ'hï iyûⁿ'ta nûⁿ-nâ'hï wïtetsatanûⁿ'ûⁿsï'. A`ne'tsâge'ta *getsatûne'litise'sti* igûⁿ'wûlstanita'sti-gwû. Utsïnâ'wa-gwû nutatanûⁿta. Nigagï' Yû!

¹ So written and pronounced by A`yûⁿini instead of utsïnä'wa

(Degâsi'sisgû'nï)--Unawa'stï e'gwa u'nitlûⁿgâ'ï. Ta'ya gû'ⁿtatï, ditsa'tista'`ti. Tsâ'l-agayû'ⁿlï yä'hä ulû'ⁿkwati-gwû nasgwû'.

Translation.

TO TREAT THE GREAT CHILL.

Listen! On high you dwell, On high you dwell--you dwell, you dwell. Forever you dwell, you anida'we, forever you dwell, forever you dwell. Relief has come--has come. Hayï!

Listen! On Ûⁿwadâ'hï you dwell, On Ûⁿwadâ'hï you dwell--you dwell, you dwell. Forever you dwell, you anida'we, forever you dwell, forever you dwell. Relief has come--has come. Hayï!

Listen! In the pines you dwell, In the pines you dwell--you dwell, you dwell. Forever you dwell, you anida'we, forever you dwell, forever you dwell. Relief has come--has come. Hayï!

Listen! In the water you dwell, In the water you dwell, you dwell, you dwell. Forever you dwell, you anida'we, forever you dwell, forever you dwell. Relief has come--has come. Hayï!

Listen! O now you have drawn near to hearken, O Little Whirlwind, O ada'wehi, in the leafy shelter of the lower mountain, there you repose. O ada'wehi, you can never fail in anything. Ha! Now rise up. A very small portion [of the disease] remains. You have come to sweep it away into the small swamp on. the upland. You have laid down your paths near the swamp. It is ordained that you shall scatter it as in play, so that it shall utterly disappear. By you it must be scattered. So shall there be relief.

Listen! O now again you have drawn near to hearken, O Whirlwind, surpassingly great. In the leafy shelter of the great mountain there you repose. O Great Whirlwind, arise quickly. A very small part [of the disease] remains. You have come to sweep the intruder into the great swamp on the upland. You have laid down your paths toward the great swamp. You shall scatter it as in play so that it shall utterly disappear. And now relief has come. All is done. Yû!

(Prescription.)--(This is to use) when they are sick with the great chill. Take a decoction of wild cherry to blow upon them. If you have Tsâ'l-agayû'ⁿlï ("old tobacco"--*Nicotiana rustica*) it also is very effective.

EXPLANATION.

Unawa'stï, "that which chills one," is a generic name for intermittent fever, otherwise known as fever and ague. It is much dreaded by the Indian doctors, who recognize several varieties of the disease, and have various theories to account for them. The above formula was obtained from A`yûⁿni (Swimmer), who described the symptoms of this variety, the "Great Chill," as blackness in the face, with alternate high fever and shaking chills. The disease generally appeared in spring or summer, and might return year after year. In the first stages the chill usually came on early in the morning, but came on later in the day as the disease progressed. There might be more than one chill during the day. There was no rule as to appetite, but the fever always produced an excessive thirst. In one instance the patient fainted from the heat and would even lie down in a stream to cool himself. The doctor believed the disease was caused by malicious tsgâ'ya, a general name for all small insects and worms, excepting intestinal worms. These tsgâ'ya--that is, the disease tsgâ'ya, not the real insects and worms--are held responsible for a large number of diseases, and in fact the tsgâ'ya doctrine is to the Cherokee practitioner what the microbe theory is to some modern scientists. The tsgâ'ya live in the earth, in the water, in the air, in the foliage of trees, in decaying wood, or wherever else insects lodge, and as they are constantly being crushed, burned or otherwise destroyed through the unthinking carelessness of the human race, they are continually actuated by a spirit of revenge. To accomplish their vengeance, according to the doctors, they "establish towns" under the skin of their victims, thus producing an irritation which results in fevers, boils, scrofula and other diseases.

The formula begins with a song of four verses, in which the doctor invokes in succession the spirits of the air, of the mountain, of the forest, and of the water. Galûⁿlatï, the word used in the first verse, signifies, as has been already explained, "on high" or "above everything," and has been used by translators to mean heaven. Ûⁿwadâ'hï in the second verse is the name of a bald mountain east of Webster, North Carolina, and is used figuratively to denote any mountains of bold outline. The Cherokees have a tradition to account

for the name, which is derived from Ûⁿwadâ'lï, "provision house."
Nâ'tsihï' in the third verse signifies "pinery," from nâ`tsï, "pine," but is
figuratively used to denote a forest of any kind.

In the recitation which follows the song, but is used only in serious
cases, the doctor prays to the whirlwind, which is considered to dwell,
among the trees on the mountain side, where the trembling of the
leaves always gives the first intimation of its presence. He declares
that a small portion of the disease still remains, the spirits invoked in
the song having already taken the rest, and calls upon the whirlwind to
lay down a path for it and sweep it away into the swamp on the
upland, referring to grassy marshes common in the small coves of the
higher mountains, which, being remote from the settlements, are
convenient places to which to banish the disease. Not satisfied with
this he goes on to direct the whirlwind to scatter the disease as it
scatters the leaves of the forest, so that it shall utterly disappear. In the
Cherokee formula the verb a`ne'tsâge'ta, means literally "to play," and
is generally understood to refer to the ball play, a`ne'tsâ, so that to a
Cherokee the expression conveys the idea of catching up the disease
and driving it onward as a player seizes the ball and sends it spinning
through the air from between his ball sticks. Niga'gï is a solemn
expression about equivalent to the Latin consummatum est.

The doctor beats up some bark from the trunk of the wild cherry and
puts it into water together with seven coals of fire, the latter being
intended to warm the decoction The leaves of Tsâl-agayû'ⁿli (Indian
tobacco--Nicotiana rustica) are sometimes used in place of the wild
cherry bark. The patient is placed facing the sunrise, and the doctor,
taking the medicine in his mouth, blows it over the body of the sick
man. First, standing between the patient and the sunrise and holding
the medicine cup in his hand, he sings the first verse in a low tone.
Then, taking some of the liquid in his mouth, he advances and blows it
successively upon the top of the head, the right shoulder, left shoulder,
and breast or back of the patient, making four blowings in all. He
repeats the same ceremony with the second, third, and fourth verse,
returning each time to his original position. The ceremony takes place
in the morning, and if necessary is repeated in the evening. It is
sometimes necessary also to repeat the treatment for several--
generally four--consecutive days.

The recitation is not used excepting in the most serious cases, when,
according to the formula, "a very small portion" of the disease still

lingers. It is accompanied by blowing *of the breath alone*, without medicine, probably in this case typical of the action of the whirlwind. After repeating the whole ceremony accompanying the song, as above described, the doctor returns to his position in front of the patient and recites in a whisper the first paragraph to the Little Whirlwind, after which he advances and blows his breath upon the patient four times as he has already blown the medicine upon him. Then going around to the north he recites the second paragraph to the Great Whirlwind, and at its conclusion blows in the same manner. Then moving around to the west--behind the patient--he again prays to the Little Whirlwind with the same ceremonies, and finally moving around to the south side he closes with the prayer to the Great Whirlwind, blowing four times at its conclusion. The medicine must be prepared anew by the doctor at the house of the patient at each application morning or evening. Only as much as will be needed is made at a time, and the patient always drinks what remains after the blowing. Connected with the preparation and care of the medicine are a number of ceremonies which need not be detailed here. The wild cherry bark must always be procured fresh; but the Tsâl-agayû'ⁿlï ("Old Tobacco") leaves may be dry. When the latter plant is used four leaves are taken and steeped in warm water with the fire coals, as above described.

THIS IS TO MAKE CHILDREN JUMP DOWN

HIÄ' TSUNSDI'GA DIL`TADI'NATANTI'YÏ. I.

Sgë! Hïsga'ya Ts`sdi'ga ha-nâ'gwa da'tûlehûⁿgû' kïlû-gwû'. Iyû'ⁿta agayû'ⁿlinasï' taya'ï. Eska'niyü unayë'histï' nûⁿta-yu'tanatï'. Sgë'! tinû'lïtgï'! Tleki'yu tsûtsestâ'gï hwïnagï'. Yû!

Sgë! Hige'cya ts`sdi'ga ha-nâ'gwa da'tûlehûⁿgû' kïlû-gwû'. Iyûⁿ'ta tsûtu'tunasï' täya'ï. Eska'niyü unayë'histï nûⁿtayu'tanatï'. Sgë! tinû'lïtgï'! Tleki'yu tsûtsestâ' hwïnagï'. Yû!

Translation.

THIS IS TO MAKE CHILDREN JUMP DOWN.

Listen! You little man, get up now at once. There comes an old woman. The horrible [old thing] is coming, only a little way off. Listen! Quick! Get your bed and let us run away. Yû!

Listen! You little woman, get up now at once. There comes your grandfather. The horrible old fellow is coming only a little way off. Listen! Quick! Get your bed and let us run away. Yû!

Explanation.

In this formula for childbirth the idea is to frighten the child and coax it to come, by telling it, if a boy, that an ugly old woman is coming, or if a girl, that her grandfather is coming only a short distance away. The reason of this lies in the fact that an old woman is the terror of all the little boys of the neighborhood, constantly teasing and frightening them by declaring that shc mcans to livc until they grow up and then compel one of them to marry her, old and shriveled as she is. For the same reason the maternal grandfather, who is always a privileged character in the family, is especially dreaded by the little girls, and nothing will send a group of children running into the house more quickly than the announcement that an old "granny," of either sex is in sight.

As the sex is an uncertain quantity, the possible boy is always first addressed in the formulas, and if no result seems to follow, the doctor then concludes that the child is a girl and addresses her in similar tones. In some cases an additional formula with the beads is used to determine whether the child will be born alive or dead. In most instances the formulas were formerly repeated with the appropriate ceremonies by some old female relative of the mother, but they are now the property of the ordinary doctors, men as well as women.

This formula was obtained from the manuscript book of A`yû'ⁿinï, who stated that the medicine used was a warm decoction of a plant called Dalâ'nige Unaste'tsï ("yellow root"--not identified), which was blown successively upon the top of the mother's head, upon the breast, and upon the palm of each hand. The doctor stands beside the woman, who is propped up in a sitting position, while repeating the first paragraph and then blows. If this produces no result he then recites the paragraph addressed to the girl and again blows. A part of the liquid is also given to the woman to drink. A`yû'ⁿinï claimed this was always effectual.

(HIÄ' TSUNSDI'GA DIL`TADI'NATANTI'YI. II.)

Hitsutsa, hitsu'tsa, tleki'yu, tleki'yu, ë'hinugâ'ï, ë'hinugâ'ï! Hi'tsu'tsa, tleki'yu, gûltsû'tï, gûltsû'tï, tinagâ'na, tinagâ'na!

Higë`yu'tsa, higë`yu'tsa, tleki'yu, tleki'yu, ë'hinugâ'ï, ë'hinugâ'ï! Higë`yu'tsa, tleki'yu, gûⁿgu'stï, gûⁿgu'stï, tinagâ'na, tinagâ'na!

Translation.

THIS IS TO MAKE CHILDREN JUMP DOWN.

Little boy, little boy, hurry, hurry, come out, come out! Little boy, hurry; a bow, a bow; let's see who'll get it, let's see who'll get it!

Little girl, little girl, hurry, hurry, come out, come out, Little girl, hurry; a sifter, a sifter; let's see who'll get it, let's see who'll get it!

Explanation.

This formula was obtained from Takwati'hï, as given to him by a specialist in this line. Takwatihi himself knew nothing of the treatment involved, but a decoction is probably blown upon the patient as described in the preceding formula. In many cases the medicine used is simply cold water, the idea being to cause a sudden muscular action by the chilling contact. In this formula the possible boy or girl is coaxed out by the promise of a bow or a meal-sifter to the one who can get it first. Among the Cherokees it is common, in asking about the sex of a new arrival, to inquire, "Is it a bow or a sifter?" or "Is it ball sticks or bread?"

TO TREAT THE BLACK YELLOWNESS

DALÂ'NI Û{ⁿ}NÄGE'Ï ADANÛ'{ⁿ}WÂTÏ.

Yuha'ahi', (yuha'ahi', yuha'ahi', yuha'ahi',)
Yuha'ahi', (yuha'ahi', yuha'ahi'), Yû!

Sgë! Û{ⁿ}tal-e'gwâhï' didultâ'hïstï ulsge'ta. Usïnu'lï dâtitu'lene'ï. Usïnu'lï dunu'y?tani'leï'.

Sgë! Ha-nâ'gwa statû'{ⁿ}gani'ga, nû{ⁿ}dâ'yï distûl`tâ'histï, Stisga'ya Dïst`sdi'ga, stida'wehi-gâgû. Û{ⁿ}tal-e'gwa dâtitulene'(ï) ulsge'ta. Usïnu'lï detïstû'l`tani'ga ulsge'ta. Ditu'talenû'{ⁿ}itsa nû{ⁿ}nâ'hï {ʷ}i'de'tutanû'{ⁿ}tatasï', nû{ⁿ}tadu'ktahû'{ⁿ}stï nige'sû{ⁿ}na. Nû'`gï iyayû'{ⁿ}latägï' ayâwe'sâlû'{ⁿ}ta de'dudûneli'sestï, Gû'{ⁿ}tsatâtagi'yû tistadi'gûlahi'sestï. Tiduda'le`nû(ï) û'{ⁿ}tale'gwâ {ʷ}itï'stûl'tati'nû{ⁿ}tani'ga. Na'`nä witûl`tâ'hïstani'ga, tadu'ktahû'{ⁿ}stï nige'sû{ⁿ}na. Ha-na'`nä {ʷ}id'ultâhiste'stï. (Yû!)

(Degasisisgû'{ⁿ}ï)--Hiä' anine'tsï ga'`tiskï adanû{ⁿ}wâtï. Ü'{ⁿ}tla atsi'la tï'`tï yï'gï.

Translation.

TO TREAT THE BLACK YELLOWNESS.

Yuha'ahi', yuha'ahi', yuha'ahi', yuha'ahi',
Yuha'ahi', yuha'ahi', yuha'ahi' Yû!

Listen! In the great lake the intruder reposes. Quickly he has risen up there. Swiftly he has come and stealthily put himself (under the sick man).

Listen! Ha! Now you two have drawn near to hearken, there in the Sun Land you repose, O Little Men, O great anida'wehi! The intruder has risen up there in the great lake. Quickly you two have lifted up the intruder. His paths have laid themselves down toward the direction whence he came. Let him never look back (toward us). When he stops to rest at the four gaps you will drive him roughly along. Now he has plunged into the great lake from which he came. There he is compelled to remain, never to look back. Ha! there let him rest. (Yû!)

(Directions.)--This is to treat them when their breast swells. Fire (coals) is not put down.

Explanation.

This formula, from A`yûⁿinï's manuscript, is used in treating a disease known as Dalâni, literally, "yellow." From the vague description of symptoms given by the doctors, it appears to be an aggravated form of biliousness, probably induced by late suppers and bad food. According to the Indian theory it is caused by revengeful animals, especially by the terrapin and its cousin, the turtle.

The doctors recognize several forms of the disease, this variety being distinguished as the "black dalâni (Dalâni Ûⁿnage'ï) and considered the most dangerous. In this form of dalânï, according to their account, the navel and abdomen of the patient swell, the ends of his fingers become black, dark circles appear about his eyes, and the throat contracts spasmodically and causes him to fall down suddenly insensible. A`yûⁿinï's method of treatment is to rub the breast and abdomen of the patient with the hands, which have been previously rubbed together in the warm infusion of wild cherry (ta'ya) bark. The song is sung while rubbing the hands together in the liquid, and the prayer is repeated while rubbing the swollen abdomen of the patient. The operation may be repeated several times on successive days.

The song at the beginning has no meaning and is sung in a low plaintive lullaby tone, ending with a sharp *Yu!* The prayer possesses a special interest, as it brings out several new points in the Cherokee mythologic theory of medicine. The "intruder," which is held to be some amphibious animal--as a terrapin, turtle, or snake--is declared to have risen up from his dwelling place in the great lake, situated toward the sunset, and to have come by stealth under the sick man. The verb implies that the disease spirit creeps under as a snake might crawl under the coverlet of a bed.

The two Little Men in the Sun Land are now invoked to drive out the disease. Who these Little Men are is not clear, although they are regarded as most powerful spirits and are frequently invoked in the formulas. They are probably the two Thunder Boys, sons of Kanati.

The Little Men come instantly when summoned by the shaman, pull out the intruder from the body of the patient, turn his face toward the sunset, and begin to drive him on by threats and blows (expressed in the word gû'ⁿtsatatagi'yû) to the great lake from which he came. On the road there are four gaps in the mountains, at each of which the disease spirit halts to rest, but is continually forced onward by his two pursuers, who finally drive him into the lake, where he is compelled to remain, without being permitted even to look back again. The four gaps are mentioned also in other formulas for medicine and the ball play and sometimes correspond with the four stages of the treatment. The direction "No fire (coals) is put down" indicates that no live coals are put into the decoction, the doctor probably using water warmed in the ordinary manner.

Takwati'hï uses for this disease a decoction of four herbs applied in the same manner. He agrees with A`yû'ⁿinï in regard to the general theory and says also that the disease may be contracted by neglecting to wash the hands after handling terrapin shells, as, for instance, the shell rattles used by women in the dance. The turtle or water tortoise (seligu'gï) is considered as an inferior being, with but little capacity for mischief, and is feared chiefly on account of its relationship to the dreaded terrapin or land tortoise (tûksï'). In Takwatihï's formula he prays to the Ancient White (the fire), of which these cold-blooded animals are supposed to be afraid, to put the fish into the water, the turtle into the mud, and to send the terrapin and snake to the hillside.

TO TREAT FOR ORDEAL DISEASES

TSUNDAYE'LIGAKTANÛ'HÏ ADANÛ'ⁿWÂTÏ

Sgë! Hanâ'gwa hatû'ⁿganiga, galû'ⁿlatï hetsadâ'histï, Kâ'lanû Û'ⁿnage, gahu'stï tsanu'lahû'ⁿsgï nige'sûⁿna. Ha-nâ'gwa (hetsatsa'ûⁿtani'ga. Hanigû'ⁿwatûⁿnigwälâe'stigwû tsalâsû'ⁿï. Asgin-u'danû higes'eï. Sanigala'gï gesû'ⁿï hastigtû'`lani'ga, duwâlu'wa'tû'tï nige'sûⁿna, nitûⁿneli'ga. Ha-Usûhi'yï wititâ'hïstani'ga. Dadu'satahû'ⁿstï nige'sûⁿna nitû'neli'ga. Utsïnä'wa nu'tatanû'ⁿta.

Sgë! Ha-nâ'gwa hatû'ⁿgani'ga, Kâ'lanû Gïgage'ï, hidawëhi'yu. Ha-gahu'stï tsanu'lahû'ⁿsgï nige'sûⁿna, etsanetse'lûhï. Ha-galûⁿlati'tsa hetsatâ'histï. Nâ'gwa hetsatsâ'ûⁿtani'ga. Nigû'ⁿwatû'ⁿnigwalâe'sti-gwû tsalâsû'ⁿï. Asgin-udanû'hi-gwû higese'ï. Ha-Sanigalâgï gesû'ⁿ hâstigû'`lani'ga ulsge'ta, ha-utsïnä'wa-gwû' nigû'ⁿtisge'stï. Usûhi'yï wïntûnë'dû. Usûhi'yï wïtitâ'hïstani'ga. Utsïnä'wa adû'ⁿni'ga.

Sgë! Ha-nâ'gwa hatû'ⁿgani'ga, Kâ'lanû Sa'ka'ni; galû'latï hetsadâ'histï, hida'wëhï. Gahu'stï tsanu'lahûⁿsgï nige'sûⁿna, etsanetse'lûhï. Ha-nâ'gwa hetsatsâ'ûⁿtani'ga. Nigû'ⁿwatû'ⁿnigwalâe'sti-gwû tsalâsû'ⁿï. Sanigalâ'gï gesû'ⁿ hastigû'`lani'ga ulsge'ta. Duwâlu'watû'tï nige'sûⁿna, nitû'neli'ga. Usûhi'yï wïtitâ'hïstani'ga, dadu'satahû'ⁿstï nige'sûⁿna nitû'neli'ga. Utsïnä'wa adû'ⁿni'ga.

Sgë! Ha-nâ'gwa hatû'ⁿgani'ga, Wa'hïlï galû'ⁿlti'tsa hetsadâ'histï, Kâ'lanû Tsûne'ga, hida'wëhï. Gahu'stï tsanul`tï nige'sûⁿna. Hanâ'gwa hetsatsâ'ûⁿtani'ga. Nigû'ⁿwatû'ⁿnigwalâe'sti-gwû tsalâsû'ⁿï. Ha-nâ'gwa detal`tani'ga. Sanigalâ'gï gesû'ⁿ, hastig'û`lani'ga ulsge'ta, duwâlu'watu'`tï nige'sûⁿna nitû'neli'ga. Usûhi'yï wïtitâ'hïstani'ga. Dadu'satahû'ⁿstï nige'sûⁿna nitû'neli'ga. Utsïnä'wa adû'ⁿni'ga.

(Dega'sisisgû'ⁿï)--Hiä' agi`li'ya unitlû'ⁿgû'ⁿï adanû'wâtï. Askwanu'tsastï'. Tsâ'l(a) Agayû'ⁿlï unitsi'lû'ⁿnû'hï gû'ⁿtatï, anû'ⁿsga`lâ'-gwû; Kanasâ'la-`nû unali'gâhû, ade'la'-`nû nû'`gi-gwû ani'gage'ï dahâ'ï, Tsâliyu'stï-`nû Usdi'ga. Gahu'sti-'`nu yuta'suyû'ⁿna sâwatu'hi-gwû atï' dawâ'hila-gwû iyû'ⁿta.

Translation.

TO TREAT FOR ORDEAL DISEASES.

Listen! Ha! Now you have drawn near to hearken and are resting directly overhead. O Black Raven, you never fail in anything. Ha! Now you are brought down. Ha! There shall be left no more than a trace upon the ground where you have been. It is an evolute ghost. You have now put it into a crevice in Sanigalagi, that it may never find the way back. You have put it to rest in the Darkening Land, so that it may never return. Let relief come.

Listen! Ha! Now you have drawn near to hearken, O Red Raven, most powerful ada'wehi. Ha! You never fail in anything, for so it was ordained of you. Ha! You are resting directly overhead. Ha! Now you are brought down. There shall remain but a trace upon the ground where you have been. It is an evolute ghost. Ha! You have put the Intruder into a crevice of Sanigalagi and now the relief shall come. It (the Intruder) is sent to the Darkening Land. You have put it to rest in the Darkening Land. Let the relief come.

Listen! Ha! Now you have drawn near to hearken, O Blue Raven; you are resting directly overhead, ada'wehi. You never fail in anything, for so it was ordained of you. Ha! Now you are brought down. There shall be left but a trace upon the ground where you have been. You have put the Intruder into a crevice in Sanigalagi, that it may never find the way back. You have put it to rest in the Darkening Land, so that it may never return. Let the relief come.

Listen! Ha! Now you have drawn near to hearken; you repose on high on Wa'hïlï, O White Raven, ada'wehi. You never fail in anything. Ha! Now you are brought down. There shall be left but a trace upon the ground where you have been. Ha! Now you have taken it up. You have put the Intruder into a crevice in Sanigalagi, that it may never find the way back. You have put it to rest in the Darkening Land, never to return. Let the relief come.

 (Directions)--This is to treat them for a painful sickness. One must suck. Use Tsâ'lagayûn'-li ("Old Tobacco"--Nicotiana rustica), blossoms, and just have them in the mouth, and Kanasâ'la (Wild Parsnip), goes with it, and four red beads also must lie there, and Tsâliyu'sti Usdi'ga ("Little (plant) Like Tobacco"--Indian Tobacco--Lobelia inflata.) And if there should be anything mixed with it (i. e., after sucking the place), just put it about a hand's-length into the mud.

Explanation.

The Cherokee name for this disease gives no idea whatever of its serious nature. The technical term, Tsundaye'liga'ktanû'hï, really refers to the enthusiastic outburst of sociability that ensues when two old friends meet. In this instance it might be rendered "an ordeal." The application of such a name to what is considered a serious illness is in accordance with the regular formulistic practice of making light of a dangerous malady in order to convey to the disease spirit the impression that the shaman is not afraid of him. A`yûⁿinï, from whom the formula was obtained, states also that the disease is sometimes sent to a man by a friend or even by his parents, in order to test his endurance and knowledge of counter spells.

As with most diseases, the name simply indicates the shaman's theory of the occult cause of the trouble, and is no clue to the symptoms, which may be those usually attendant upon fevers, indigestion, or almost any other ailment.

In some cases the disease is caused by the conjurations of an enemy, through which the patient becomes subject to an inordinate appetite, causing him to eat until his abdomen is unnaturally distended. By the same magic spells tobacco may be conveyed into the man's body, causing him to be affected by faintness and languor. The enemy, if bitterly revengeful, may even put into the body of his victim a worm or insect (tsgâya), or a sharpened stick of black locust or "fat" pine, which will result in death if not removed by a good doctor. Sometimes a weed stalk is in some occult manner conveyed into the patient's stomach, where it is transformed into a worm. As this disease is very common, owing to constant quarrels and rival jealousies, there are a number of specialists who devote their attention to it.

The prayer is addressed to the Black, Red, Blue, and White Ravens, their location at the four cardinal points not being specified, excepting in the case of the white raven of Wa'hilï, which, as already stated, is said to be a mountain in the south, and hence is used figuratively to mean the south. The ravens are each in turn declared to have put the disease into a crevice in Sanigala'gi--the Cherokee name of Whiteside Mountain, at the head of Tuckasegee River, in North Carolina, and used figuratively for. any high precipitous mountain--and to have left no more than a trace upon the ground where it has been. The adjective translated "evolute" (udanûhï) is of frequent occurrence in the formulas. but has no exact equivalent in English. It signifies springing into being or life from an embryonic condition. In this instance it would imply that whatever object the enemy has put into the body of the sick man has there developed into a ghost to trouble him.

The directions are expressed in a rather vague manner, as is the case with most of A`yûⁿini's attempts at original composition. The disease is here called by another name, agi`li'ya unitlûⁿgû'ⁿï, signifying "when they are painfully sick." The treatment consists in sucking the part most affected, the doctor having in his mouth during the operation the blossoms of Tsâ'l-agayû'ⁿlï (Nicotiana rustica), Kanasâ'la (wild parsnip,) and Tsâliyusti Usdiga (Lobelia inflata.) The first and last of these names signify "tobacco" and "tobacco-like," while the other seems to contain the same word, tsâ'la, and the original idea may have been to counteract the witchcraft by the use of the various species of "tobacco," the herb commonly used to drive away a witch or wizard. During the sticking process four red beads lie near upon a piece of (white) cloth, which afterward becomes the perquisite of the doctor. Though not explicitly stated, it is probable that the doctor holds in his mouth a decoction of the blossoms named, rather than the blossoms themselves. On withdrawing his mouth from the spot and ejecting the liquid into a bowl, it is expected that there will be found "mixed" with it a small stick, a pebble, an insect, or something of the kind, and this the shaman then holds up to view as the cause of the disease. It is afterward buried a "hand's length" (awâ'hilû)[1] deep in the mud. No directions were given as to diet or tabu.

---

[1] This word, like the expression "seven days," frequently has a figurative meaning. Thus the sun is said to be seven awâ'hilû above the earth

CONCERNING HUNTING

GÛNÂ'HILÛ'ⁿTA UGÛ'ⁿWA`LÏ.

Una'lelü' eskiska'l`tasï'. Iskwa'lelü eskiska'l`tasï'. Yû! Ela-Kana'tï tsûldâ'hïstû'ⁿ, tsûwatsi'la astû'ⁿ detsatasi'ga. Ts?skwâ'lï uda'nisä`'testï, ugwala'ga udu'yaheti'dege'stï. Sunûsi'ya-gwû udanisä`'testï, ts`su'lti-gwû nige'sûⁿna.

Hïkayû'ⁿlï Gi'gage-gâgû', tsine'tsï gesû'ⁿ aw`stitege'stï. *Tsästû' utatiyi*, nâ'gwa *tsäs`tû gasû'hisä`ti atisge'sti*. Ha-nâ'gwa nûⁿnâ tsusdi' tutana'wa-tegû' *digana'watû'ⁿta* atisge'stï. Utalï' udaniû'hï ugwala'ga gûⁿwatuy'ahïti'tege'stï, hïlahiyû'ⁿta-gwû ʷustû'`stï nige'sûⁿna. D?stiskwâ'lï deudû'nisä`te'stï. Yû!

Translation.

CONCERNING HUNTING.

Give me the wind. Give me the breeze. Yû! O Great Terrestrial Hunter, I come to the edge of your spittle where you repose. Let your stomach cover itself; let it be covered with leaves. Let it cover itself at a single bend, and may you never be satisfied.

And you, O Ancient Red, may you hover above my breast while I sleep. Now let good (dreams?) develop; let my experiences be propitious. Ha! Now let my little trails be directed, as they lie down in various directions(?). Let the leaves be covered with the clotted blood, and may it never cease to be so. You two (the Water and the Fire) shall bury it in your stomachs. Yû!

Explanation.

This is a hunting formula, addressed to the two great gods of the hunter, Fire and Water. The evening before starting the hunter "goes to water," as already explained, and recites the appropriate formula. In the morning he sets out, while still fasting, and travels without eating or drinking until nightfall. At sunset he again goes to water, reciting this formula during the ceremony, after which he builds his camp fire, eats his supper and lies down for the night, first rubbing his breast with ashes from the fire. In the morning he starts out to look for game.

"Give me the wind," is a prayer that the wind may be in his favor, so that the game may not scent him. The word rendered here "Great Terrestrial Hunter," is in the original "Ela-Kana'tï." In this *e'la* is the earth and *kana'tï* is a term applied to a successful hunter. The great Kanatï, who, according to the myth, formerly kept all the game shut up in his underground caverns, now dwells above the sky, and is frequently invoked by hunters. The raven also is often addressed as Kanatï in these hunting formulas. Ela-Kana'tï, the Great Terrestrial Hunter--as distinguished from the other two--signifies the river, the name referring to the way in which the tiny streams and rivulets search out and bring down to the great river the leaves and débris of the mountain forests. In formulas for medicine, love, the ball play, etc., the river is always addressed as the Long Person (Yû'ⁿwï Gûnahi'ta). The "spittle" referred to is the foam at the edge of the water. "Let your stomach be covered with leaves" means, let the blood-stained leaves where the stricken game shall fall be so numerous as to cover the surface of the water. The hunter prays also that sufficient game may be found in a single bend of the river to accomplish this result without the necessity of searching through the whole forest, and to that end he further prays that the river may never be satisfied, but continually longing for more. The same idea is repeated in the second paragraph, The hunter is supposed to feed the river with blood washed from the game. In like manner he feeds the fire, addressed in the second paragraph as the "Ancient Red," with a piece of meat cut from the tongue of the deer. The prayer that the fire may hover above his breast while he sleeps and brings him favorable dreams, refers to his rubbing his breast with ashes from his camp fire before lying down to sleep, in order that the fire may bring him dream omens of success for the morrow. The Fire is addressed either as the Ancient White or the Ancient Red, the allusion in the first case being to the light or the ashes of the fire; in the other case, to the color of the burning coals. "You two shall bury it in your stomachs" refers to the bloodstained leaves and the piece of meat which are cast respectively into the river and the fire. The formula was obtained from A`yûⁿinï, who explained it in detail.

THIS IS FOR HUNTING BIRDS

HIÄ' TSI'SKWA GANÂHILIDASTI'YÏ.

Tsïgë'! Hïkayû'ⁿl-Une'ga, tsûltâ'histû'ⁿ gûlitâ'hïstani'ga. Nâ'gwa tsûda'ntâ talehï'sani'ga. Sâ'gwa igûnsi'ya ts?skwâlï' udû'nisate'stï, ts?su'ltï nige'sûⁿna. Wane'(ï) tigi'gage(ï) tali'kanëli'ga. Uⁿtalï udanû'hï tsägista'`tï.

Hïkayû'ⁿl-Une'ga, *anu'ya uwâtatâ'gï agi'stï tätsiskâ'ltane'lûhï.* Uⁿtalï u'danû' *te'tûlskew?si'ga.*

Hïkayû'ⁿl-Une'ga, nûⁿnâ'(hï) kana'tï skwatetâ'stani'ga. Unigwalû'ⁿgï te'gatûⁿtsi'ga. Nûⁿnâ'(hï) kana'tï tati'kiyû'ⁿgwita'watise'stï. Unigwalû'ⁿgï tigû'ⁿwatû'tsanû'hï.

Hïkayû'ⁿl-Une'ga, Kana'tï, sk?salatâ'titege'stï, sa`ka'ni ginu't?tï nige'sûⁿna. Sgë!

Translation.

THIS IS FOR HUNTING BIRDS.

Listen! O Ancient White, where you dwell in peace I have come to rest. Now let your spirit arise. Let it (the game brought down) be buried in your stomach, and may your appetite never be satisfied. The red hickories have tied themselves together. The clotted blood is your recompense.

O Ancient White, * * * Accept the clotted blood (?).

O Ancient White. put me in the successful hunting trail. Hang the mangled things upon me. Let me come along the successful trail with them doubled up (under my belt). It (the road) is clothed with the mangled things.

O Ancient White, O Kanati, support me continually, that I may never become blue. Listen!

Explanation.

This formula, from A`yûⁿinï's manuscript, is recited by the bird-hunter in the morning while standing over the fire at his hunting camp before starting out for the day's hunt. A`yû'ⁿini stated that seven blowgun arrows are first prepared, including a small one only a "hand-length" (awâ'hilû) long. On rising in the morning the hunter, standing over the fire, addresses it as the "Ancient White," rubbing his hands together while repeating the prayer. He then sets out for the hunting ground, where he expects to spend the day, and on reaching it he shoots away the short arrow at random, without attempting to trace its flight. There is of course some significance attached to this action and perhaps an accompanying prayer, but no further information upon this point was obtainable. Having shot away the magic arrow, the hunter utters a peculiar hissing sound, intended to call up the birds, and then goes to work with his remaining arrows. On all hunting expeditions it is the regular practice, religiously enforced, to abstain from food until sunset.

A favorite method with the bird-hunter during the summer season is to climb a gum tree, which is much frequented by the smaller birds on account of its berries, where, taking up a convenient position amid the branches with his noiseless blowgun and arrows, he deliberately shoots down one bird after another until his shafts are exhausted, when he climbs down, draws out the arrows from the bodies of the birds killed, and climbs up again to repeat the operation. As the light darts used make no sound, the birds seldom take the alarm, and are too busily engaged with the berries to notice their comrades dropping to the ground from time to time, and pay but slight attention even to the movements of the hunter.

The prayer is addressed to the Ancient White (the Fire), the spirit most frequently invoked by the hunter, who, as before stated, rubs his hands together over the fire while repeating the words. The expressions used are obscure when taken alone, but are full of meaning when explained in the light of the hunting customs. The "clotted blood" refers to the bloodstained leaves upon which the fallen game has lain. The expression occurs constantly in the hunting formulas. The hunter gathers up these bloody leaves and casts them upon the fire, in order to draw omens for the morrow from the manner in which they burn. A part of the tongue, or some other portion of the animal, is usually cast upon the coals also for the same purpose. This subject will be treated at length in a future account of the hunting ceremonies.

"Let it be buried in your stomach" refers also to the offering made the fire. By the red hickories are meant the strings of hickory bark which the bird hunter twists about his waist for a belt. The dead birds are carried by inserting their heads under this belt. Red is, of course, symbolic of his success. "The mangled things" (unigwalû'ⁿgï) are the wounded birds. Kana'tï is here used to designate the fire, on account of its connection with the hunting ceremonies.

TO SHOOT DWELLERS IN THE WILDERNESS

INAGË'HÏ AYÂSTIⁿYÏ.

Usïnuli'yu Selagwû'tsï Gigage'ï getsû'ⁿneliga tsûdandâgi'hï aye`li'yu, usïnuli'yu. Yû!

Translation.

TO SHOOT DWELLERS IN THE WILDERNESS.

Instantly the Red Selagwû'tsï strike you in the very center of your soul--instantly. Yû!

Explanation.

This short formula, obtained from A`wani'ta, is recited by the hunter while taking aim. The bowstring is let go--or, rather, the trigger is pulled--at the final *Yû!* He was unable to explain the meaning of the word selagwû'tsï further than that it referred to the bullet. Later investigation, however, revealed the fact that this is the Cherokee name of a reed of the genus Erianthus, and the inference follows that the stalk of the plant was formerly used for arrow shafts. Red implies that the arrow is always successful in reaching the mark aimed at, and in this instance may refer also to its being bloody when withdrawn from the body of the animal. Inagë'hï, "dwellers in the wilderness," is the generic term for game, including birds, but A`wani'ta has another formula intended especially for deer.

BEAR SONG

(YÂ'NA TÏ'KANÂGI'TA.)

He +! Hayuya'haniwä', hayuya'haniwä', hayuya'haniwä',
hayuya'haniwä'.
Tsistuyi' nehandu'yanû, Tsistuyi' nehandu'yanû--Yoho' +!
He +! Hayuya'haniwä', hayuya'haniwä', hayuya'haniwä',
hayuya'haniwä'.
Kuwâhi' nehandu'yanû', Kuwâhi nehandu'yanû--Yoho' +!
He +! Hayuya'haniwä', hayuya'haniwä', hayuya'haniwä,
hayuya'haniwä'.
Uyâ`ye' nehandu'yanû, Uyâ`ye' nehandu'yanû'--Yoho' +!
He +! Hayuya'haniwä', hayuya'haniwä', hayuya'haniwä,
hayuya'haniwä'.
Gâtekwâ'(hï) nehandu'yanû, Gâtekwâ'(hï) nehandu'yanû'--Yoho' +!
Ûlë-`nû' asëhï' tadeya'statakûnï' gû^{n}nage astû'tsïkï'.

Translation.

BEAR SONG.

He! Hayuya'haniwä', hayuya'haniwä', hayuya'haniwä', hayuya'haniwä'.
   In Rabbit Place you were conceived (repeat)--Yoho' +!
He! Hayuya'haniwä', hayuya'haniwä', hayuya'haniwä', hayuya'haniwä'.
   In Mulberry Place you were conceived (repeat)--Yoho' +!
He! Hayuya'haniwä', hayuya'haniwä', hayuya'haniwä', hayuya'haniwä'.
   In Uyâ'`yë you were conceived (repeat)--Yoho' +!
He! Hayuya'haniwä', hayuya'haniwä', hayuya'haniwä', hayuya'haniwä'.
   In the Great Swamp (?) you were conceived (repeat)--Yoho' +!
And now surely we and the good black things, the best of all, shall see
each other.

Explanation.

This song, obtained from A`yû'^{n}inï in connection with the story of the
Origin of the Bear, as already mentioned, is sung by the bear hunter, in
order to attract the bears, while on his way from the camp to the place
where he expects to hunt during the day. It is one of those taught the
Cherokees by the Ani-Tsâ'kahï before they lost their human shape and
were transformed into bears. The melody is simple and plaintive.

The song consists of four verses followed by a short recitation. Each verse begins with a loud prolonged *He +!* and ends with *Yoho' +!* uttered in the same manner. Hayuya'haniwä' has no meaning. Tsistu'yï, Kuwâ'hï, Uyâ'`yë, and Gâte'kwâhï are four mountains, in each of which the bears have a townhouse and hold a dance before going into their dens for the winter. The first three named are high peaks in the Smoky Mountains, on the Tennessee line, in the neighborhood of Clingman's Dome and Mount Guyot. The fourth is southeast of Franklin, North Carolina, toward the South Carolina line, and may be identical with Fodderstack Mountain. In Kuwahi dwells the great bear chief and doctor, in whose magic bath the wounded bears are restored to health. They are said to originate or be conceived in the mountains named, because these are their headquarters. The "good black things" referred to in the recitation are the bears.

THIS IS FOR CATCHING LARGE FISH

HIÄ' ATSÛ`TI'YÏ TSUN'TANÛ.

Sgë! Nâ'gwa hitsatû'ⁿgani'ga hitsiga'tugï'. Titsila'wisû'ⁿhï ᵘwâgi'`lï tege'tsûts`gû'`lawïstï'. Tsuli'stana'lû ûlë' waktûï, agi'stï une'ka itsû'ⁿyatanilû'ïstani'ga. Gûⁿwatu'hwïtû' nûⁿna'hï degûndâltsi'dâhe'stï. ᵘWâ'hisâ'nahï tigiwatsi'la. Tutsegû'`lawistï'tege'stï. Ûⁿtalï' degû'ⁿwatanûhï, uhisa'`tï nige'sûⁿna. Tsuwatsi'la dadâl`tsi'ga. A`yû A`yû'ⁿinï tigwadâ'ita. Yû!

Translation.

THIS IS FOR CATCHING LARGE FISH.

Listen! Now you settlements have drawn near to hearken. Where you have gathered in the foam you are moving about as one. You Blue Cat and the others, I have come to offer you freely the white food. Let the paths from every direction recognize each other. Our spittle shall be in agreement. Let them (your and my spittle) be together as we go about. They (the fish) have become a prey and there shall be no loneliness. Your spittle has become agreeable. I am called Swimmer. Yû!

Explanation.

This formula, from A`yûⁿini's' book, is for the purpose of catching large fish. According to his instructions, the fisherman must first chew a small piece of Yugwilû' (Venus' Flytrap--Dionæa muscipula) and spit it upon the bait and also upon the hook. Then, standing facing the stream, he recites the formula and puts the bait upon the hook. He will be able to pull out a fish at once, or if the fish are not about at the moment they will come in a very short time.

The Yugwilû' is put upon the bait from the idea that it will enable the hook to attract and hold the fish as the plant itself seizes and holds insects in its cup. The root is much prized by the Cherokees for this purpose, and those in the West, where the plant is not found, frequently send requests for it to their friends in Carolina.

The prayer is addressed directly to the fish, who are represented as living in settlements. The same expression as has already been mentioned is sometimes used by the doctors in speaking of the *tsgâ'ya* or worms which are supposed to cause sickness by getting under the skin of the patient. The Blue Cat (*Amiurus, genus*) is addressed as the principal fish and the bait is spoken of as the "white food," an expression used also of the viands prepared at the feast of the green corn dance, to indicate their wholesome character. "Let the paths from every direction recognize each other," means let the fishes, which are supposed to have regular trails through the water, assemble together at the place where the speaker takes his station, as friends recognizing each other at a distance approach to greet each other, ᵘWâhisâ'nahï tigiwatsi'la, rendered "our spittle shall be in agreement," is a peculiar archaic expression that can not be literally translated. It implies that there shall be such close sympathy between the fisher and the fish that their spittle shall be as the spittle of one individual. As before stated, the spittle is believed to exert an important influence upon the whole physical and mental being. The expression "your spittle has become agreeable" is explained by A`yûⁿinï as an assertion or wish that the fish may prove palatable, while the words rendered "there shall be no loneliness" imply that there shall be an abundant catch.

CONCERNING LIVING HUMANITY (LOVE)

LOVE.

(YÛⁿWË'HÏ UGÛ'ⁿWA`LÏ I.)

Ku! Sgë! *Alahi'yï* tsûl`dâ'histï, Higë`'ya tsûl`di'yï,
hatû'ⁿgani'ga. *Elahi'yï* iyû'ⁿta ditsûl`dâ'histï, Higë`'ya Tsûne'ga. Tsisa'`tï
nige'sûⁿna. Tsâduhi'yï. Nâ'gwa-skïn'ï usïnuli'yu hûⁿskwane'`lûⁿgû'
tsisga'ya agine'ga. Agisa'`tï nige'sûⁿna. Nâ'gwa nû'ⁿnâ une'ga
hûⁿskwanûⁿneli'ga. Uhisa'`tï nige'sûⁿna. Nâ'gwa skwade'tastani'ga.
Sa`ka'ni u'tatï nige'sûⁿna. Nûⁿnâ une'ga skiksa'`ûⁿtaneli'ga. Elaye'`lï
iyû'ⁿta skwalewistä'`tani'ga E'latï gesû'ⁿ tsïtage'stï. Agisa'`tï nige'sûⁿna.
Agwâ'duhi'yu. Kûltsâ'te une'ga skiga'`tani'ga. Uhisa'`tï nige'sûⁿna,
gûⁿkwatsâti'tege'sti. Tsi-sa`ka'ni agwä'tï nige'sûⁿna. Usïnuli'yu
hûⁿskwane'`lûⁿgû'.

Ha-nâ'gwûlë *Elahi'yï* iyû'ⁿtä dûhiyane'`lûⁿgû' a'gë'`ya sa`ka'ni. Nâ'gwa
nûⁿnâ'hï sa`ka'ni hûⁿtane'`laneli'ga. Uhisa'`tï-gwû u'danû dudusa'gï
tanela'sï. Nûⁿnâ'hï sa`ka'nï tade'tâstani'ga. Nâgwûlë'
hûⁿhiyatsâ'ûⁿtaniga. E'latï gesû'ⁿ tû'l`taniga. Dedu'laskû'ⁿ-gwû
igû'ⁿwa`lawï'stï uhi'sa`ti'yï widaye'la`ni'ga. Dedulaskû'ⁿ-gwû
igû'ⁿwa`lawï'stï uhi'sa`ti'yï nitû'ⁿneli'ga.

Ha-sâgwahi'yu itsilasta'agï + + uwä'sahi'yu, etsane'`laneli'ga. Agisa'`tï
nige'sûⁿna. Agwâ'duhï. A'yû agwadantâ'gï aye`li'yu d?ka'`lani'lï
duda'ntâ, uktahû'ⁿstï nige'sûⁿna. Yû'ⁿwï tsu'tsatûⁿ widudante'`tï
nige'sûⁿna, nitû'ⁿneli'ga. Sâ'gwahï itsilasta'lagï, etsane'`laneli'ga
kûlkwâ'gi-nasï' igûlstû'`lï gegane'`lanû'ⁿ.

Anisga'ya anewadi'stûⁿ unihisa`ti'yï. Tsu'nada'neilti'yï. Dï'la-gwû
degû'ⁿwänatsegû'`lawi'sdidegû'. Ayâ'ise'ta-gwû u'danû.
Tsunada'neilti'yï. Utse'tsti-gwû degû'ⁿwänatsegû'`lawis'didegû'.
Tsunada'neilti'yï. Ka'ga-gwû degû'ⁿwänatsegû'`awisdidegû'.
Tsunada'neilti'yï. Da'l`ka-gwû degû'ⁿwänatsegû'`lawisdidegû'.

Kûlkwâ'gï igûlsta'lagï unihisa`ti'yu. Ige'ski-gwû nige'sû'ⁿna. Ayâ'ise'ta-
gwû u'danû degû'ⁿwänatsûn`ti-degû'. K?si-gwû degû'ⁿwänatsûn`ti-
degû'. A'yagâgû' tsisga'ya agine'ga ûⁿgwane'`lanû'hï + + Nûⁿdâgû'ⁿyï
iti'tsa ditsidâ'ga. Agisa'`tï nige'sûⁿna. Agwâduhi'yu. Tsi-sa`ka'nï
agwä'tatï nige'sûⁿna. Kûltsâ'te une'ga ûⁿni'tagâgû' gûkwatsâ'nti-degû'.

Agisä'`tï nige'sûⁿna. A'yû agwadantâ'gï aye`li'yu gûlasi'ga tsûda'ntâ, uktahû'ⁿstï nige'sûⁿna. A'yû tsï'gï tsûda'nta O O. Sgë!

Translation.

CONCERNING LIVING HUMANITY (LOVE).

Kû! Listen! In Alahi'yï you repose, O Terrible Woman, O you have drawn near to hearken. There in Elahiyï you are at rest, O White Woman. No one is ever lonely when with you. You are most beautiful. Instantly and at once you have rendered me a white man. No one is ever lonely when with me. Now you have made the path white for me. It shall never be dreary. Now you have put me into it. It shall never become blue. You have brought down to me from above the white road. There in mid-earth (mid-surface) you have placed me. I shall stand erect upon the earth. No one is ever lonely when with me. I am very handsome. You have put me into the white house. I shall be in it as it moves about and no one with me shall ever be lonely. Verily, I shall never become blue. Instantly you have caused it to be so with me.

And now there in Elahiyï you have rendered the woman blue. Now you have made the path blue for her. Let her be completely veiled in loneliness. Put her into the blue road. And now bring her down. Place her standing upon the earth. Where her feet are now and wherever she may go, let loneliness leave its mark upon her. Let her be marked out for loneliness where she stands.

Ha! I belong to the (Wolf) (+ +) clan, that one alone which was allotted into for you. No one is ever lonely with me. I am handsome. Let her put her soul the very center of my soul, never to turn away. Grant that in the midst of men she shall never think of them. I belong to the one clan alone which was allotted for you when the seven clans were established.

Where (other) men live it is lonely. They are very loathsome. The common polecat has made them so like himself that they are fit only for his company. They have became mere refuse. They are very loathsome. The common opossum has made them so like himself that they are fit only to be with him. They are very loathsome. Even the crow has made them so like himself that they are fit only for his company. They are very loathsome. The miserable rain-crow has made them so like himself that they are fit only to be with him.

The seven clans all alike make one feel very lonely in their company. They are not even good looking. They go about clothed with mere refuse. They even go about covered with dung. But I--I was ordained to be a white man. I stand with my face toward the Sun Land. No one is ever lonely with me. I am very handsome. I shall certainly never become blue. I am covered by the everlasting white house wherever I go. No one is ever lonely with me. Your soul has come into the very center of my soul, never to turn away. I--(Gatigwanasti,) (O O)--I take your soul. Sgë!

Explanation.

This unique formula is from one of the loose manuscript sheets of Gatigwanasti, now dead, and belongs to the class known as Yûⁿwë'hï or love charms (literally, concerning "living humanity") including all those referring in any way to the marital or sexual relation. No explanation accompanies the formula, which must therefore be interpreted from analogy. It appears to be recited by the lover himself--not by a hired shaman--perhaps while painting and adorning himself for the dance. (*See next two formulas.*)

The formula contains several obscure expressions which require further investigation. Elahiyï or Alahiyï, for it is written both ways in the manuscript, does not occur in any other formula met with thus far, and could not be explained by any of the shamans to whom it was submitted. The nominative form may be Elahï, perhaps from *ela*, "the earth," and it may be connected with Wa'hïlï, the formulistic name for the south. The spirit invoked is the White Woman, white being the color denoting the south.

Uhisaʻˋtï, rendered here "lonely," is a very expressive word to a Cherokee and is of constant recurrence in the love formulas. It refers to that intangible something characteristic of certain persons which inevitably chills and depresses the spirits of all who may be so unfortunate as to come within its influence. Agisaʻˋtï nige'sûⁿna, "I never render any one lonely," is an intensified equivalent for, "I am the best company in the world," and to tell a girl that a rival lover is uhisaʻˋtï is to hold out to her the sum of all dreary prospects should she cast in her lot with him.

The speaker, who evidently has an exalted opinion of himself, invokes the aid of the White Woman, who is most beautiful and is never uhisaʻtï. She at once responds by making him a white--that is, a happy--man, and placing him in the white road of happiness, which shall never become blue with grief or despondency. She then places him standing in the middle of the earth, that he may be seen and admired by the whole world, especially by the female portion. She finally puts him into the white house, where happiness abides forever. The verb implies that the house shelters him like a cloak and goes about with him wherever he may go.

There is something comical in the extreme self-complacency with which he asserts that he is very handsome and will never become blue and no one with him is ever lonely. As before stated, white signifies peace and happiness, while blue is the emblem of sorrow and disappointment.

Having thus rendered himself attractive to womankind, he turns his attention to the girl whom he particularly desires to win. He begins by filling her soul with a sense of desolation and loneliness. In the beautiful language of the formula, her path becomes blue and she is veiled in loneliness. He then asserts, and reiterates, that he is of the one only clan which was allotted for her when the seven clans were established.

He next pays his respects to his rivals and advances some very forcible arguments to show that she could never be happy with any of them. He says that they are all "lonesome" and utterly loathsome--the word implies that they are mutually loathsome--and that they are the veriest trash and refuse. He compares them to so many polecats, oppossums, and crows, and finally likens them to the raincrow (cuckoo; *Coccygus*), which is regarded with disfavor on account of its disagreeable note. He grows more bitter in his denunciations as he proceeds and finally disposes of the matter by saying that all the seven clans alike are uhisaʻtï and are covered with filth. Then follows another glowing panegyric of himself, closing with the beautiful expression, "your soul has come into the very center of mine, never to turn away," which reminds one forcibly of the sentiment in the German love song, "Du liegst mir im Herzen." The final expression, "I take your soul," implies that the formula has now accomplished its purpose in fixing her thoughts upon himself.

When successful, a ceremony of this kind has the effect of rendering the victim so "blue" or lovesick that her life is in danger until another formula is repeated to make, her soul "white" or happy again. Where the name of the individual or clan is mentioned in these formulas the blank is indicated in the manuscript by crosses + + or ciphers O O or by the word iyu'stï, "like."

THIS TELLS ABOUT GOING INTO THE WATER

HI'Ä ÄMA'YÏ Ä'TAWAST'YÏ KANÂ'HEHÛ.

Sgë! Ha-nâ'gwa usïnuli'yu hatû'ⁿgani'ga *Higë'`yagu'ga*, tsûwatsi'la gi'gage tsiye'la skïna'dû`'lani'ga. O O digwadâ'ita. Sa`ka'nï tûgwadûne'lûhï. Atsanû'ⁿgï gi'gage skwâsû'hisa`tani'ga. + + kûlstä'lagï + sa'ka'nï nu'tatanû'ⁿta. Ditu'nûⁿnâ'gï dagwû'laskû'ⁿ-gwû deganu'y`tasi'ga. Galâ'nûⁿtse'ta-gwû dagwadûne'lidise'stï. Sgë!

Translation.

THIS TELLS ABOUT GOING INTO THE WATER.

Listen! O, now instantly, you have drawn near to hearken, O Agë'`yagu'ga. You have come to put your red spittle upon my body. My name is (Gatigwanasti.) The blue had affected me. You have come and clothed me with a red dress. She is of the (Deer) clan. She has become blue. You have directed her paths straight to where I have my feet, and I shall feel exultant. Listen!

Explanation.

This formula, from Gatigwanasti's book, is also of the Yûⁿwë'hï class, and is repeated by the lover when about to bathe in the stream preparatory to painting himself for the dance. The services of a shaman are not required, neither is any special ceremony observed. The technical word used in the heading, ä'tawasti'yï, signifies plunging or going entirely into a liquid. The expression used for the ordinary "going to water," where the water is simply dipped up with the hand, is ämâ'yï dita`ti'yï, "taking them to water."

The prayer is addressed to Agë'`yaguga, a formulistic name for the moon, which is supposed to exert a great influence in love affairs, because the dances, which give such opportunities for love making, always take place at night. The shamans can not explain the meaning of the term, which plainly contains the word agë'`ya, "woman," and may refer to the moon's supposed influence over women. In Cherokee mythology the moon is a man. The ordinary name is nû'ⁿdâ, or more fully, nû'ⁿdâ sûⁿnâyë'hï, "the sun living in the night," while the sun itself is designated as nû'ⁿndâ igë'hï, "the sun living in the day."

By the red spittle of Agë'`yagu'ga and the red dress with which the lover is clothed are meant the red paint which he puts upon himself. This in former days was procured from a deep red clay known as ela-wâ'tï, or "reddish brown clay." The word red as used in the formula is emblematic of success in attaining his object, besides being the actual color of the paint. Red, in connection with dress or ornamentation, has always been a favorite color with Indians throughout America, and there is some evidence that among the Cherokees it was regarded also as having a mysterious protective power. In all these formulas the lover renders the woman blue or disconsolate and uneasy in mind as a preliminary to fixing her thoughts upon himself. (*See next formula.*)

SONG FOR PAINTING

(YÛ'ⁿWË'HÏ UGÛ'ⁿWA`LÏ II.)

Yû'ⁿwëhï, yû'ⁿwëhï, yû'ⁿwëhï, yû'ⁿwëhï.
Galû'ⁿlatï, datsila'ï--Yû'ⁿwëhï, yû'ⁿwëhï, yû'ⁿwëhï, yû'ⁿwëhï.
Nûⁿdâgû'ⁿyï gatla'ahï--Yû'ⁿwëhï.

Gë`yagu'ga Gi'gage, tsûwatsi'la gi'gage tsiye'la skïna'dû`lani'ga--
Yû'ⁿwëhï, yû'ⁿwëhï, yû'ⁿwëhï.

Hiä-`nû' atawe'ladi'yï kanâ'hëhû galûⁿlti'tla.

Translation.

SONG FOR PAINTING.

Yû'ⁿwëhï, yû'ⁿwëhï, yû'ⁿwëhï, yû'ⁿwëhï.
I am come from above--Yû'ⁿwëhï, yû'ⁿwëhï, yû'ⁿwëhï, yû'ⁿwëhï.
I am come down from the Sun Land--yû'ⁿwëhï.

O Red Agë`yagu'ga. you have come and put your red spittle upon my
body--Yû'ⁿwëhï, yû'ⁿwëhï, yû'ⁿwëhï!.

And this above is to recite while one is painting himself.

Explanation.

This formula, from Gatigwanasti, immediately follows the one last
given, in the manuscript book, and evidently comes immediately after
it also in practical use. The expressions used have been already
explained. The one using the formula first bathes in the running
stream, reciting at the same time the previous formula "Amâ'yï
Ä'tawasti'yï." He then repairs to some convenient spot with his paint,
beads, and other paraphernalia and proceeds to adorn himself for the
dance, which usually begins about an hour after dark, but is not fairly
under way until nearly midnight. The refrain, yû'ⁿwëhï, is
probably *sung* while mixing the paint, and the other portion is recited
while applying the pigment, or vice versa. Although these formula are
still in use, the painting is now obsolete, beyond an occasional daubing

of the face, without any plan or pattern, on the occasion of a dance or ball play.

TO ATTRACT AND FIX THE AFFECTIONS

ADALANI'STA`TI'YÏ. I.

Sgë! Ha-nâ'gwa hatû'ⁿgani'ga nihï'--

--Tsa'watsi'lû tsïkï' tsïkû' ayû'.
--Hiyelû' tsïkï' tsïkû' ayû'.
--Tsäwiyû' tsïkï' tsïkû' ayû'.
--Tsûnahu' tsïkï' tsïkû' ayû'.

Sgë! Nâ'gwa hatû'ⁿgani'ga, Hïkayû'ⁿlige. Hiä' asga'ya uda'ntâ tsa`ta'hisi'ga [Hïkayû'ⁿlige] hiye'lastûⁿ. Tsaskûlâ'hïsti-gwû' nige'sûⁿna. Dïkana'watûⁿta-gwû tsûtû'neli'ga. Hïlû dudantë`tï nige'sûⁿna. Duda'ntâ dûskalûⁿ'tseli'ga. Astï' digû'ⁿnage tagu'talûⁿtani'ga.

Translation.

TO ATTRACT AND FIX THE AFFECTIONS.

Listen! O, now you have drawn near to hearken--

--Your spittle, I take it, I eat it.
--Your body, I take it, I eat it.
--Your flesh, I take it, I eat it
--Your heart, I take it, I eat it

Each sung four times.

Listen! O, now you have drawn near to hearken, O, Ancient One. This man's (woman's) soul has come to rest at the edge of your body. You are never to let go your hold upon it. It is ordained that you shall do just as you are requested to do. Let her never think upon any other place. Her soul has faded within her. She is bound by the black threads.

Explanation.

This formula is said by the young husband, who has just married an especially engaging wife, who is liable to be attracted by other men. The same formula may also be used by the woman to fix her husband's affections. On the first night that they are together the husband watches until his wife is asleep, when, sitting up by her side, he recites the first words: Sgë! Ha-nâ'gwa hatû'^{n}gani'ga nihï', and then sings the next four words: Tsawatsi'lû tsïkï' tsïkû' ayû', "Your spittle, I take it, I eat it," repeating the words four times. While singing he moistens his fingers with spittle, which he rubs upon the breast of the woman. The next night he repeats the operation, this time singing the words, "I take your body." The third night, in the same way, he sings, "I take your flesh," and the fourth and last night, he sings "I take your heart," after which he repeats the prayer addressed to the Ancient One, by which is probably meant the Fire (the Ancient White). A`yû^{n}inï states that the final sentences should be masculine, i. e., His soul has faded, etc., and refer to any would-be seducer. There is no gender distinction in the third person in Cherokee. He claimed that this ceremony was so effective that no husband need have any fears for his wife after performing it.

FOR SEPARATION (OF LOVERS)

ADAYE'LIGA'GTA`TÏ'.

Yû! Galû'ⁿlatï tsûl`dâ'histï, Giya'giya' Sa'ka'ni, nâ'gwa nûⁿtalûⁿ i'yû'ⁿta. Tsâ'la Sa`ka'ni tsûgistâ'`tï adûⁿni'ga. Nâ'gwa nidâtsu'l`tanû'ⁿta, nû'ⁿtâtagû' hisa'hasi'ga. Tani'dâgûⁿ' aye'`lï dehidâ'siga. Unada'ndâ dehiyâ'staneli'ga. Nidugale'ntanû'ⁿta nidûhûⁿneli'ga.

Tsisga'ya agine'ga', nûⁿdâgû'ⁿyï ditsidâ'`stï. Gû'nï âstû' uhisa'`tï nige'sûⁿna. Agë'`ya une'ga hi'ä iyu'stï gûlstû'`lï, iyu'sti tsûdâ'ita. Uda'ndâ usïnu'lï dâdatinilû'gûⁿelï'. Nûⁿdâgû'ⁿyitsû' dâdatinilugûstanelï. Tsisga'ya agine'ga, ditsidûstû'ⁿï nû`nû' kana'tlani'ga. Tsûnkta' tegä`la'watege'stï. Tsiye'lûⁿ gesû'ⁿï uhisa'`tï nige'sûⁿna.

Translation.

FOR SEPARATION (OF LOVERS).

Yû! On high you repose, O Blue Hawk, there at the far distant lake. The blue tobacco has come to be your recompense. Now you have arisen at once and come down. You have alighted midway between them where they two are standing. You have spoiled their souls immediately. They have at once become separated.

I am a white man; I stand at the sunrise. The good sperm shall never allow any feeling of loneliness. This white woman is of the Paint (iyustï) clan; she is called (iyustï) Wâyï'. We shall instantly turn her soul over. We shall turn it over as we go toward the Sun Land. I am a white man. Here where I stand it (her soul) has attached itself to (literally, "come against") mine. Let her eyes in their sockets be forever watching (for me). There is no loneliness where my body is.

Explanation.

This formula, from A`yûninï's book, is used to separate two lovers or even a husband and wife, if the jealous rival so desires. In the latter case the preceding formula, from the same source, would be used to forestall this spell. No explanation of the ceremony is given, but the reference to tobacco may indicate that tobacco is smoked or thrown into the fire during the recitation. The particular hawk invoked (giya'giya') is a large species found in the coast region but seldom met with in the mountains. Blue indicates that it brings trouble with it, while white in the second paragraph indicates that the man is happy and attractive in manner.

In the first part of the formula the speaker calls upon the Blue Hawk to separate the lovers and spoil their souls, *i. e.*, change their feeling toward each other. In the second paragraph he endeavors to attract the attention of the woman by eulogizing himself. The expression, "we shall turn her soul over," seems here to refer to turning her affections, but as generally used, to turn one's soul is equivalent to killing him.

TO FIX THE AFFECTIONS

(ADALANÏ'STÄ`TIYÏ II.)

Yû! Ha-nâ'gwa ada'ntï dätsâsi'ga, * * hïlû(stû'`lï), (* *) ditsa-(dâ'ita).
A'yû O O tsila(stû'`lï). Hiye'la tsïkï' tsïkû'. (Yû!).

Yû! Ha-nâ'gwa ada'ntï dätsâsi'ga, * * hïlû(stû'`lï), (* *) ditsa-(dâ'ita).
A'yû O O tsûwi'ya tsïkï' tsïkû'. Yû!

Yû! Ha-nâ'gwa ada'ntï dätsâsi'ga, * * hïlû(stû'`lï), (* *) ditsa-(dâ'ita).
A'yû O O tsûwatsi'la tsïkï' tsïkû'. Yû!

Yû! Ha-nâ'gwa ada'ntï dätsâsi'ga, * * hïlû(stû'`lï), (* *) ditsa-(dâ'ita).
A'yû O O tsûnahü' tsïkï' tsïkû'. Yû!

Sgë! "Ha-nâ'gwa ada'ntï dutsase', tsugale'ntï nige'sû'ⁿna," tsûdûneï,
Hïkayû'ⁿlige galû'ⁿlatï. Kananë'skï Û'ⁿnage galû'ⁿlatï
(h)etsatsâ'ûⁿtänile'ï. Tsänilta'gï tsûksâ'ûⁿtanile'ï. * * gûla(stû'`lï), * *
ditsadâ'(ita). Dudantâ'gï uhani'latâ tïkwenû'ⁿtani'ga. Kûlkwâ'gï
igûlsta'lagï iyû'ⁿta yû'ⁿwï adayû'ⁿlatawä' dudûne'lida'lûⁿ uhisa'`tï
nige'sûⁿna.

Sgë! Ha-nâ'gwatï uhisa'`tï dutlû'ⁿtani'ga. Tsû'nkta daskâ'lûⁿtsi'ga.
Sâ'gwahï di'kta de'gayelûⁿtsi'ga. Ga'tsa igûnû'nugâ'ïstû uda'ntâ?
Usû'hita nudanû'ⁿna ûltûⁿge'ta, gûⁿwadûneli'dege'stï. Igûⁿwûlsta'`ti-
gwû duwâlu'wa`tûⁿtï nige'sûⁿna. Kananë'skï Û'ⁿnage'ï tsanildew`se'stï
ada'ntâ uktûⁿlesi'dastï nige'sûna. Gadâyu'stï tsûdâ'ita ada'ntï
tside'atsasi'ga. A'ya a'kwatseli'ga.

Sgë! Ha-nâ'gwûlë' hûⁿhatûⁿga'ga, Hïkayû'ⁿlï Gi'gage. Tsetsûli'sï
hiye'lastûⁿ a`ta'hisi'ga. Ada'ntâ hasû'gû'`lawï'stani'ga, tsa'skaláhistï
nige'sûⁿna. Hïkayû'ⁿlige denätsegû`la'wïstani'ga. Agë'`ya
gï'nsûⁿgû`lawïs'tani'ga uda'ntâ *uwahisï'sata*. Dïgïnaskûlâ'hïstï
nige'sûⁿna. Yû!

Hi'ä nasgwû' u`tlâ'yi-gwû dïgalû'ⁿwistan'tï snûⁿâ'yï
hani'`lihûgûnasgi'stï. Gane'tsï aye'`lï asi'tadis'tï watsi'la, ganûⁿli'yetï
aguwaye'nï andisgâ'ï. Sâi'yï tsika'nâhe itsu'laha'gwû.

Translation.

TO FIX THE AFFECTIONS.

Yû! Ha! Now the souls have come together. You are of the Deer (x x) clan. Your name is (x x) Ayâsta, I am of the Wolf (o-o) clan. Your body, I take it, I eat it. Yû! Ha! Now the souls have come together. You are of the Deer clan. Your name is Ayâsta. I am of the Wolf clan. Your flesh I take, I eat. Yû!

Yû! Ha! Now the souls have come together. You are of the Deer clan. Your name is Ayâsta. I am of the Wolf clan. Your spittle I take, I eat. I! Yû!

Yû! Ha! Now the souls have come together. You are of the Deer clan. Your name is Ayâsta. I am of the Wolf clan. Your heart I take, I eat. Yû!

Listen! "Ha! Now the souls have met, never to part," you have said, O Ancient One above. O Black Spider, you have been brought down from on high. You have let down your web. She is of the Deer clan; her name is Ayâsta. Her soul you, have wrapped up in (your) web. There where the people of the seven clans are continually coming in sight and again disappearing (i. e. moving about, coming; and going), there was never any feeling of loneliness.

Listen! Ha! But now you have covered her over with loneliness. Her eyes have faded. Her eyes have come to fasten themselves on one alone. Whither can her soul escape? Let her be sorrowing as she goes along, and not for one night alone. Let her become an aimless wanderer, whose trail may never be followed. O Black Spider, may you hold her soul in your web so that it shall never get through the meshes. What is the name of the soul? They two have come together. It is mine!

Listen! Ha! And now you have hearkened, O Ancient Red. Your grandchildren have come to the edge of your body. You hold them yet more firmly in your grasp, never to let go your hold. O Ancient One, we have become as one. The woman has put her (x x x) soul into our hands. We shall never let it go! Yû!

(Directions.)--And this also is for just the same purpose (the preceding formula in the manuscript book is also a love charm). It must be done by stealth at night when they are asleep. One must put the hand on the middle of the breast and rub on spittle with the hand, they say. The other formula is equally good.

Explanation.

This formula to fix the affections of a young wife is taken from the manuscript sheets of the late Gatigwanasti. It very much resembles the other formula for the same purpose, obtained from A`yû'ⁿinï, and the brief directions show that the ceremony is alike in both. The first four paragraphs are probably sung, as in the other formula, on four successive nights, and, as explained in the directions and as stated verbally by A`yû'ⁿinï, this must be done. stealthily at night while the woman is asleep, the husband rubbing his spittle on her breast with his hand while chanting the song in a low tone, hardly above a whisper. The prayer to the Ancient One, or Ancient Red (Fire), in both formulas, and the expression, "I come to the edge of your body," indicate that the hands are first warmed over the fire, in accordance with the general practice when laying on the hands. The prayer to the Black Spider is a beautiful specimen of poetic imagery, and hardly requires an explanation. The final paragraph indicates the successful accomplishment of his purpose. "Your grandchildren" (tsetsûli'sï) is an expression frequently used in addressing the more important deities.

TO SHORTEN A NIGHT-GOER ON THIS SIDE

SÛⁿNÂ'YÏ EDÂ'HÏ E'SGA ASTÛⁿTI'YÏ.

Sgë! Uhyûⁿtsâ'yï galûnlti'tla tsûltâ'histï, Hïsgaya Gigage'ï, usïnu'lï di'tsakûnï' denatlûⁿhi'sani'ga, Uy-igawa'stï duda'ntï. Nûⁿnâ'hï tatuna'watï. Usïnu'lï duda'ntâ dani'yûⁿstanilï'.

Sgë! Uhyûⁿtlâ'yï galûⁿlti'tla tsûltâ'histï, Hïsga'ya Të'halu, *hinaw?sü'?ki*. Ha-usïnu'lï nâ'gwa di'tsakûnï' denatlûⁿhisani'ga uy-igawa'stï duda'ntï. Nûⁿnâ'hï tätuna'wätï. Usïnu'lï duda'ntâ dani'galïstanï'.

Translation.

TO SHORTEN A NIGHT-GOER ON THIS SIDE.

Listen! In the Frigid Land above you repose, O Red Man, quickly we two have prepared your arrows for the soul of the Imprecator. He has them lying along the path. Quickly we two will take his soul as we go along.

Listen! In the Frigid Land above you repose, O Purple Man, * * * *. Ha! Quickly now we two have prepared your arrows for the soul of the Imprecator. He has them lying along the path. Quickly we two will cut his soul in two.

Explanation.

This formula, from A`yû'ⁿinïs' book, is for the purpose of driving away a witch from the house of a sick person, and opens up a most interesting chapter of Cherokee beliefs. The witch is supposed to go about chiefly under cover of darkness, and hence is called sûⁿnâ'yï edâ'hï, "the night goer." This is the term in common use; but there are a number of formulistic expressions to designate a witch, one of which, u'ya igawa'stï, occurs in the body of the formula and may be rendered "the imprecator," i. e., the sayer of evil things or curses. As the counteracting of a deadly spell always results in the death of its author, the formula is stated to be not merely to drive away the wizard, but to kill him, or, according to the formulistic expression, "to shorten him (his life) on this side."

When it becomes known that a man is dangerously sick the witches front far and near gather invisibly about his house after nightfall to worry him and even force their way in to his bedside unless prevented by the presence of a more powerful shaman within the house. They annoy the sick man and thus hasten his death by stamping upon the roof and beating upon the sides of the house; and if they can manage to get inside they raise up the dying sufferer from the bed and let him fall again or even drag him out upon the floor. The object of the witch in doing this is to prolong his term of years by adding to his own life as much as he can take from that of the sick man. Thus it is that a witch who is successful in these practices lives to be very old. Without going into extended details, it may be sufficient to state that the one most dreaded, alike by the friends of the sick man and by the lesser witches, is the Kâ'lana-ayeli'skï or Raven Mocker, so called because he flies through the air at night in a shape of fire, uttering sounds like the harsh croak of a raven.

The formula here given is short and simple as compared with some others. There is evidently a mistake in regard to the Red Man, who is here placed in the north, instead of in the east, as it should be. The reference to the arrows will be explained further on. Purple, mentioned in the second paragraph, has nearly the same symbolic meaning as blue, viz: Trouble, vexation and defeat; hence the Purple Man is called upon to frustrate the designs of the witch.

To drive away the witch the shaman first prepares four sharpened sticks, which he drives down into the ground outside the house at each of the four corners, leaving the pointed ends projecting upward and outward. Then, about noontime he gets ready the Tsâl-agayû'ⁿlï or "Old Tobacco" (*Nicotiana rustica*), with which he fills his pipe, repeating this formula during the operation, after which he wraps the pipe thus filled in a black cloth. This sacred tobacco is smoked only for this purpose. He then goes out into the forest, and returns just before dark, about which time the witch may be expected to put in an appearance. Lighting his pipe, he goes slowly around the house, puffing the smoke in the direction of every trail by which the witch might be. able to approach, and probably repeating the same or another formula the while. He then goes into the house and awaits results. When the witch approaches under cover of the darkness, whether in his own proper shape or in the form of some animal, the sharpened stick on that side of the house shoots up into the air and comes down like an arrow upon his head, inflicting such a wound as proves fatal within seven days. This explains the words of the formula, "We have prepared your arrows for the soul of the Imprecator. He has them lying along the path". A`yû'ⁿinï said nothing about the use of the sharpened sticks in this connection, mentioning only the tobacco, but the ceremony, as here described, is the one ordinarily used. When wounded the witch utters a groan which is heard by those listening inside the house, even at the distance of half a mile. No one knows certainly who the witch is until a day or two afterward, when some old man or woman, perhaps in a remote settlement, is suddenly seized with a mysterious illness and before seven clays elapse is dead.

I HAVE LOST SOMETHING

GAHU'STÏ A'GIYAHU'SA.

Sgë! Ha-nâ'gwa hatû'ⁿgani'ga Nû'ⁿya Wâtige'ï, gahu'stï tsûtska'dï nige'sûⁿna. Ha-nâ'gwa dû'ⁿgihya'lï. Agiyahu'sa sï'kwa, haga' tsûⁿ-nû' iyû'ⁿta dätsi'waktû'hï. Tla-`ke' a'ya a'kwatseli'ga. O O digwadâi'ta.

Translation.

I HAVE LOST SOMETHING.

Listen! Ha! Now you have drawn near to hearken, O Brown Rock; you never lie about anything. Ha! Now I am about to seek for it. I have lost a hog and now tell me about where I shall find it. For is it not mine? My name is ------------.

Explanation.

This formula, for finding anything lost, is so simple as to need but little explanation. Brown in this instance has probably no mythologic significance, but refers to the color of the stone used in the ceremony. This is a small rounded water-worn pebble, in substance resembling quartz and of a reddish-brown color. It is suspended by a string held between the thumb and finger of the shaman, who is guided in his search by the swinging of the pebble, which, according to their theory, will swing farther in the direction of the lost article than in the contrary direction! The shaman, who is always fasting, repeats the formula, while closely watching the motions of the swinging pebble. He usually begins early in the morning, making the first trial at the house of the owner of the lost article. After noting the general direction toward which it seems to lean he goes a considerable distance in that direction, perhaps half a mile or more, and makes a second trial. This time the pebble may swing off at an angle in another direction. He follows up in the direction indicated for perhaps another half mile, when on a third trial the stone may veer around toward the starting point, and a fourth attempt may complete the circuit. Having thus arrived at the conclusion that the missing article is somewhere within a certain circumscribed area, he advances to the center of this space and marks out upon the ground a small circle inclosing a cross with arms pointing toward the four cardinal points. Holding the stone over the center of the cross he again repeats the formula and notes the direction in which the pebble swings. This is the final trial and he fiow goes slowly and carefully over the whole surface in that direction, between the center of the circle and the limit of the circumscribed area until in theory, at least, the article is found. Should he fail, he is never at a loss for excuses, but the specialists in this line are generally very shrewd guessers well versed in the doctrine of probabilities.

There are many formulas for this purpose, some of them being long and elaborate. When there is reason to believe that the missing article has been stolen, the specialist first determines the clan or settlement to which the thief belongs and afterward the name of the individual. Straws, bread balls, and stones of various kinds are used in the different formulas, the ceremony differing according to .the medium employed. The stones are generally pointed crystals or antique arrowheads, and are suspended as already described, the point being supposed to turn finally in the direction of the missing object. Several of these stones have been obtained on the reservation and are now deposited in the National Museum. It need excite no surprise to find the hog mentioned in the formula, as this animal has been domesticated among the Cherokees for more than a century, although most of them are strongly prejudiced against it.

THIS IS TO FRIGHTEN A STORM

HIA' UNÁLE (ATEST'YÏ).

Yuhahi', yuhahi', yuhahi', yuhahi', yuhahi',
Yuhahi', yuhahi', yuhahi', yuhahi', yuhahi'--Yû!

Sgë! Ha-nâ'gwa hïnahû^n'ski tayï'. Ha-tâ'sti-gwû gû^{n}ska'ihû. Tsûtali'i-gwati'na halu'ʻnï. Kû'nigwati'na dula'ska galû'^{n}lati-gwû witu'ktï. Wigû^{n}yasë'hïsï. Â'talï tsugû'^{n}yï wite'tsatanû'^{n}û^{n}sï' nû^{n}nâhï tsane'lagï de'gatsana'wadise'stï. Kûnstû' dutsasû'^{n}ï atû'^{n}wasûtë'hahï' tsûtûneli'sestï. Sgë!

Translation.

THIS IS TO FRIGHTEN A STORM.

Yuhahi', yuhahi', yuhahi', yuhahi', yuhahi',
Yuhahi', yuhahi', yuhahi', yuhahi', yuhahi'--Yû!

Listen! O now you are coming in rut. Ha! I am exceedingly afraid of you. But yet you are only tracking your wife. Her footprints can be seen there directed upward toward the heavens. I have pointed them out for you. Let your paths stretch out along the tree tops (?) on the lofty mountains (and) you shall have them (the paths) lying down without being disturbed, Let (your path) as you go along be where the waving branches meet. Listen!

Explanation.

This formula, from A`yû'^{n}inï's book, is for driving away, or "frightening" a storm, which threatens to injure the growing corn. The first part is a meaningless song, which is sting in a low tone in the peculiar style of most of the sacred songs. The storm, which is not directly named, is then addressed and declared to be coming on in a fearful manner on the track of his wife, like an animal in the rutting season. The shaman points out her tracks directed toward the upper regions and begs the storm spirit to follow her along the waving tree tops of the lofty mountains, where he shall be undisturbed.

The shaman stands facing the approaching storm with one hand stretched out toward it. After repeating the song and prayer he gently blows in the direction toward which he wishes it to go, waving his hand in the same direction as though pushing away the storm. A part of the storm is usually sent into the upper regions of the atmosphere. If standing at the edge of the field, he holds a blade of corn in one hand while repeating the ceremony.

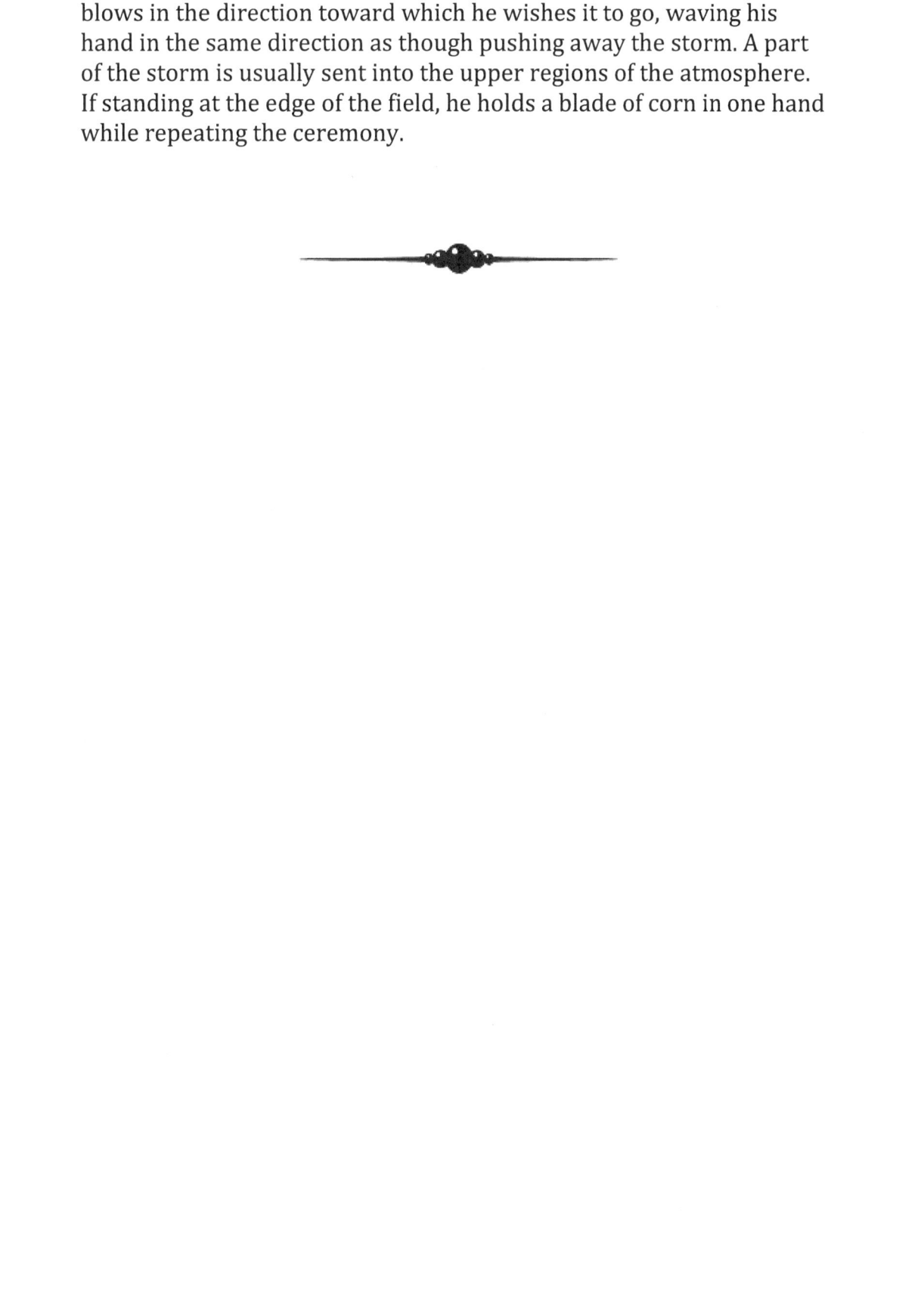

WHAT THOSE WHO HAVE BEEN TO WAR DID TO HELP THEMSELVES

DANAWÛ' TSUNEDÂLÛ'HÏ NUNATÛ'NELI'TALÛ'ⁿHÏ U'NALSTELTA`'TANÛ'HÏ.

Hayï'! Yû! Sgë! Nâ'gwa usïnuli'yu A'tasu Gi'gage'ï hinisa'latani'ga. Usïnu'lï duda'ntâ u'nanugâ'tsidastï' nige'sûⁿna. Duda'ntâ e`lawi'nï iyû'ⁿta ä'tasû digûⁿnage'ï degûⁿlskwï'tahise'stï, anetsâge'ta unanugâ'istï nige'sûⁿna, nitinû'ⁿneli'ga. Ä'tasû dusa'ladanû'ⁿstï nige'sûⁿna, nitinû'ⁿneli'ga. E`lawi'nï iyû'ⁿta ä'tasû ûⁿnage' ugûⁿ'hatû ûⁿnage' sâ'gwa da`liyë'kû`lani'ga *unadutlâ'gï*. Unanugâ'tsida'stï nige'sûⁿna, nûⁿneli'ga.

Usïnuli'yu tsunada'ntâ kûl`kwâ'gine tigalû'nltiyû'ⁿï iyû'ⁿta ada'ntâ tega'yë`ti'tege'stï. Tsunada'ntâ tsuligalï'stï nige'sûⁿna dudûni'tege'stï. Usïnu'lï deniû'ⁿeli'ga galû`ⁿlati iyû'ⁿta widu'l`tâhïsti'tege'stï. Ä'tasû gigage'ï dëhatagû'ⁿyastani'ga. Tsunada'ntâ tsudastû'nilida'stï nige'sûⁿna nûⁿneli'ga. Tsunada'ntâ galû'ⁿlatï iyû'ⁿta witë`'titege'stï. Tsunada'ntâ anigwalu'gï une'ga gûⁿwa'nadagû'ⁿyastitege'stï. Sa`ka'nï udûnû'hï nige'sûⁿna usïnuli'yu. Yû!

Translation.

WHAT THOSE WHO HAVE BEEN TO WAR DID TO HELP THEMSELVES.

Hayï'! Yû! Listen! Now instantly we have lifted up the red war club. Quickly his soul shall be without motion. There under the earth, where the black war clubs shall be moving about like ball sticks in the game, there his soul shall be, never to reappear. We cause it to be so. He shall never go and lift up the war club. We cause it to be so. There under the earth the black war club (and) the black fog have come together as one for their covering. It shall never move about (i. e., the black fog shall never be lifted from them). We cause it to be so.

Instantly shall their souls be moving about there in the seventh heaven. Their souls shall never break in two. So shall it be. Quickly we have moved them (their souls) on high for them, where they shall be going about in peace. You (?) have shielded yourselves (?) with the red war club. Their souls shall never be knocked about. Cause it to be so.

There on high their souls shall be going about. Let them shield themselves with the white war whoop. Instantly (grant that) they shall never become blue. Yû!

Explanation.

This formula, obtained from A`wani'ta, may be repeated by the doctor for as many as eight men at once when about to go to war. It is recited for four consecutive nights, immediately before setting out. There is no tabu enjoined and no beads are used, but the warriors "go to water" in the regular way, that is, they stand at the edge of the stream, facing the east and looking down upon the water, while the shaman, standing behind them, repeats the formula. On the fourth night the shaman gives to each man a small charmed root which has the power to confer invulnerability. On the eve of battle the warrior after bathing in the running stream chews a portion of this and spits the juice upon his body in order that the bullets of the enemy may pass him by or slide off from his skin like drops of water. Almost every man of the three hundred East Cherokees who served in the rebellion had this or a similar ceremony performed before setting out--many of them also consulting the oracular ulû'ⁿsû'tï stone at the same time--and it is but fair to state that not more than two or three of the entire number were wounded in actual battle.

In the formula the shaman identifies himself with the warriors, asserting that "we" have lifted up the red war club, red being the color symbolic of success and having no reference to blood, as might be supposed from the connection. In the first paragraph he invokes curses upon the enemy, the future tense verb *It shall be*, etc., having throughout the force of *let it be*. He puts the souls of the doomed enemy in the lower regions, where the black war clubs are constantly waving about, and envelops them in a black fog, which shall never be lifted and out of which they shall never reappear. From the expression in the second paragraph, "their souls shall never be knocked about," the reference to the black war clubs moving about like ball sticks in the game would seem to imply that they are continually buffeting the doomed souls under the earth. The spirit land of the Cherokees is in the west, but in these formulas of malediction or blessing the soul of the doomed man is generally consigned to the underground region, while that of the victor is raised by antithesis to the seventh heaven.

Having disposed of the enemy, the shaman in the second paragraph turns his attention to his friends and at once raises their souls to the seventh heaven, where they shall go about in peace, shielded by (literally, "covered with") the red war club of success, and never to be knocked about by the blows of the enemy. "Breaking the soul in two" is equivalent to snapping the thread of life, the soul being regarded as an intangible something having length, like a rod or a string. This formula, like others written down by the same shaman, contains several evident inconsistencies both as to grammar and mythology, due to the fact that A`wanita is extremely careless with regard to details and that this particular formula has probably not been used for the last quarter of a century. The warriors are also made to shield themselves with the white war whoop, which should undoubtedly be the red war whoop, consistent with the red war club, white being the color emblematic of peace, which is evidently an incongruity. The war whoop is believed to have a positive magic power for the protection of the warrior, as well as for terrifying the foe.

The mythologic significance of the different colors is well shown in this formula. Red, symbolic of success, is the color of the war club with which the warrior is to strike the enemy and also of the other one with which he is to shield or "cover" himself. There is no doubt that the war whoop also should be represented as red. In conjuring with the beads for long life, for recovery from sickness, or for success in love, the ball play, or any other undertaking, the red beads represent the party for whose benefit the magic spell is wrought, and he is figuratively clothed in red and made to stand upon a red cloth or placed upon a red seat. The red spirits invoked always live in the east and everything pertaining to them is of the same color.

Black is always typical of death, and in this formula the soul of the enemy is continually beaten about by black war clubs and enveloped in a black fog. In conjuring to destroy an enemy the shaman uses black beads and invokes the black spirits--which always live in the west-- bidding them tear out the man's soul, carry it to the west, and put it into the black coffin deep in the black mud, with a black serpent coiled above it.

Blue is emblematic of failure, disappointment, or unsatisfied desire. "They shall never become blue" means that they shall never fail in anything they undertake. In love charms the lover figuratively covers himself with red and prays that his rival shall become entirely blue and walk in a blue path. The formulistic expression, "He is entirely blue," closely approximates in meaning the common English phrase, "He feels blue." The blue spirits live in the north.

White--which occurs in this formula only by an evident error--denotes peace and happiness. In ceremonial addresses, as at the green corn dance and ball play, the people figuratively partake of white food and after the dance or the game return along the white trail to their white houses. In love charms the man, in order to induce the woman to cast her lot with his, boasts "I am a white man," implying that all is happiness where he is. White beads have the same meaning in the bead conjuring and white was the color of the stone pipe anciently used in ratifying peace treaties. The white spirits live in the south (Wa'halä).

Two other colors, brown and yellow, are also mentioned in the formulas. Wâtige'ï, "brown," is the term used to include brown, bay, dun, and similar colors, especially as applied to animals. It seldom occurs in the formulas and its mythologic significance is as yet undetermined. Yellow is of more frequent occurrence and is typical of trouble and all manner of vexation, the yellow spirits being generally invoked when the shaman wishes to bring down calamities upon the head of his victim, without actually destroying him. So far as present knowledge goes, neither brown nor yellow can be assigned to any particular point of the compass.

Usïnuli'yu, rendered "instantly," is the intensive form of usïnu'lï "quickly," both of which words recur constantly in the formulas, in some entering into almost every sentence. This frequently gives the translation an awkward appearance. Thus the final sentence above, which means literally "they shall never become blue instantly," signifies "Grant that they shall never become blue, i. e., shall never fail in their purpose, *and grant our petition instantly*."

TO DESTROY LIFE

DIDA'LATLI'`TĬ.

Sgë! Nâ'gwa tsûdantâ'gï tegû'ⁿyatawâ'ilateli'ga. Iyustï (O O) tsilastû'`lï Iyu'stï (O O) ditsadâ'ita. Tsûwatsi'la elawi'nï tsidâ'hïstani'ga. Tsûdantâgï elawi'nï tsidâ'hïstani'ga. Nû'ⁿya gû'ⁿnage gûⁿyu'tlûⁿtani'ga. Ä`nûwa'gï gû'ⁿnage' gûⁿyû'tlûⁿtani'ga. Sûⁿ'talu'ga gû'ⁿnage degû'ⁿyanu'galû'ⁿtani'ga, tsû'nanugâ'istï nige'sûⁿna. Usûhi'yï nûnⁿnâ'hï wite'tsatanû'ⁿûⁿsï gûne'sâ gû'ⁿnage asahalagï'. Tsûtû'neli'ga. Elawâ'tï asa'halagï'a'dû'ni'ga. Usïnuli'yu Usûhi'yï gûltsâ'të digû'ⁿnagesta'yï, elawâ'tï gû'ⁿnage tidâ'hïstï wa`yanu'galûⁿtsi'ga. Gûne'sa gû'ⁿage sûⁿtalu'ga gû'ⁿnage gayu'tlûⁿtani'ga. Tsûdantâ'gï ûska'lûⁿtsi'ga. Sa`ka'nï adû'ⁿni'ga. Usû'hita atanis'se'tï, ayâ'lâtsi'sestï tsûdantâ'gï, tsû'nanugâ'istï nige'sûⁿna. Sgë!

Translation.

TO DESTROY LIFE.

Listen! Now I have come to step over your soul. You are of the (wolf) clan. Your name is (A`yû'ⁿinï). Your spittle I have put at rest under the earth. Your soul I have put at rest under the earth. I have come to cover you over with the black rock. I have come to cover you over, with the black cloth. I have come to cover you with the black slabs, never to reappear. Toward the black coffin of the upland in the Darkening Land your paths shall stretch out. So shall it be for you. The clay of the upland has come (to cover you). (?) Instantly the black clay has lodged there where it is at rest at the black houses in the Darkening Land. With the black coffin and with the black slabs I have come to cover you. Now your soul has faded away. It has become blue. When darkness comes your spirit shall grow less and dwindle away, never to reappear. Listen!

Explanation.

This formula is from the manuscript book of A`yû'ⁿinï, who explained the whole ceremony. The language needs but little explanation. A blank is left for the name and clan of the victim, and is filled in by the shaman. As the purpose of the ceremony is to bring about the death of the victim, everything spoken of is symbolically colored black, according to the significance of the colors as already explained. The declaration near the end, "It has become blue," indicates that the victim now begins to feel in himself the effects of the incantation, and that as darkness comes on his spirit will shrink and gradually become less until it dwindles away to nothingness.

When the shaman wishes to destroy the life of another, either for his own purposes or for hire, he conceals himself near the trail along which the victim is likely to pass. When the doomed man appears the shaman waits until he has gone by and then follows him secretly until he chances to spit upon the ground. On coming up to the spot the shaman collects upon the end of a stick a little of the dust thus moistened with the victim's spittle. The possession of the man's spittle gives him power over the life of the man himself. Many ailments are said by the doctors to be due to the fact that some enemy has by this means "changed the spittle" of the patient and caused it to breed animals or sprout corn in the sick man's body. In the love charms also the lover always figuratively "takes the spittle" of the girl in order to fix her affections upon himself. The same idea in regard to spittle is found in European folk medicine.

The shaman then puts the clay thus moistened into a tube consisting of a joint of the Kanesâ'la or wild parsnip, a poisonous plant of considerable importance in life-conjuring ceremonies. He also puts into the tube seven earthworms beaten into a paste, and several splinters from a tree which has been struck by lightning. The idea in regard to the worms is not quite clear, but it may be that they are expected to devour the soul of the victim as earthworms are supposed to feed upon dead bodies, or perhaps it is thought that from their burrowing habits they may serve to hollow out a grave for the soul under the earth, the quarter to which the shaman consigns it. In other similar ceremonies the dirt-dauber wasp or the stinging ant is buried in the same manner in order that it may kill the soul, as these are said to kill other more powerful insects by their poisonous sting or bite. The wood of a tree struck by lightning is also a potent spell for both good and evil and is used in many formulas of various kinds.

Having prepared the tube, the shaman goes into the forest to a tree which has been struck by lightning. At its base he digs a hole, in the bottom of which he puts a large yellow stone slab. He then puts in the tube, together with seven yellow pebbles, fills in the earth and finally builds a fire over the spot to destroy all traces of his work. The yellow stones are probably chosen as the next best substitute for black stones, which are not always easy to find. The formula mentions "black rock," black being the emblem of death, while yellow typifies trouble. The shaman and his employer fast until after the ceremony.

If the ceremony has been properly carried out, the victim becomes blue, that is, he feels the effects in himself at once, and, unless he employs the countercharms of some more powerful shaman, his soul begins to shrivel up and dwindle, and within seven days he is dead. When it is found that the spell has no effect upon the intended victim it is believed that he has discovered the plot and has taken measures for his own protection, or that, having suspected a design against him--as, for instance, after having won a girl's affections from a rival or overcoming him in the ball play--he has already secured himself from all attempts by counterspells. It then becomes a serious matter, as, should he succeed in turning the curse aside from himself, it will return upon the heads of his enemies.

The shaman and his employer then retire to a lonely spot in the mountains, in the vicinity of a small stream, and begin a new series of conjurations with the beads. After constructing a temporary shelter of bark laid over poles, the two go down to the water, the shaman taking with him two pieces of cloth, a yard or two yards in length, one white, the other black, together with seven red and seven black beads. The cloth is the shaman's pay for his services, and is furnished by his employer, who sometimes also supplies the beads. There are many formulas for conjuring with the beads, which are used on almost all important occasions, and differences also in the details of the ceremony, but the general practice is the same in all cases. The shaman selects a bend in the river where his client can look toward the east while facing up stream. The man then takes up his position on the bank or wades into the stream a short distance, where--in the ceremonial language--the water is a "hand length" (*awâ'hilû*) in depth and stands silently with his eyes fixed upon the water and his back to the shaman on the bank. The shaman then lays upon the ground the two pieces of cloth, folded into convenient size, and places the red beads--typical of success and his client--upon the white cloth, while the black beads--emblematic of death and the intended victim--are laid upon the black cloth. It is probable that the first cloth should properly be red instead of white, but as it is difficult to get red cloth, except in the shape of handkerchiefs, a substitution has been made, the two colors having a close mythologic relation. In former days a piece of buckskin and the small glossy seeds of the Viper's Bugloss (*Echium vulgare*) were used instead of the cloth and beads. The formulistic name for the bead is *sû'nïkta*, which the priests are unable to analyze, the ordinary word for beads or coin being *adélâ*.

The shaman now takes a red bead, representing his client, between the thumb and index finger of his right hand, and a black bead, representing the victim, in like manner, in his left hand. Standing a few feet behind his client he turns toward the east, fixes his eyes upon the bead between the thumb and finger of his right hand, and addresses it as the Sû'nïkta Gigäge'ï, the Red Bead, invoking blessings upon his client and clothing him with the red garments of success. The formula is repeated in a low chant or intonation, the voice rising at intervals, after the manner of a revival speaker. Then turning to the black bead in his left hand he addresses it in similar manner, calling down the most withering curses upon the head of the victim. Finally looking up he addresses the stream, under the name of Yû'ⁿwï Gûnahi'ta, the "Long Person," imploring it to protect his client and raise him to the seventh heaven, where he will be secure from all his enemies. The other, then stooping down, dips up water in his hand seven times and pours it upon his head, rubbing it upon his shoulders and breast at the same time. In some cases he dips completely under seven times, being stripped, of course, even when the water is of almost icy coldness. The shaman, then stooping down, makes a small hole in the ground with his finger, drops into it the fatal black bead, and buries it out of sight with a stamp of his foot. This ends the ceremony, which is called "taking to water."

While addressing the beads the shaman attentively observes them as they are held between the thumb and finger of his outstretched hands. In a short time they begin to move, slowly and but a short distance at first, then faster and farther, often coming down as far as the first joint of the finger or even below, with an irregular serpentine motion from side to side, returning in the same manner. Should the red bead be more lively in its movements and come down lower on the finger than the black bead, he confidently predicts for the client the speedy accomplishment of his desire. On the other hand, should the black bead surpass the red in activity, the spells of the shaman employed by the intended victim are too strong, and the whole ceremony must be gone over again with an additional and larger quantity of cloth. This must be kept up until the movements of the red beads give token of success or until they show by their sluggish motions or their failure to move down along the finger that the opposing shaman can not be overcome. In the latter case the discouraged plotter gives up all hope, considering himself as cursed by every imprecation which he has unsuccessfully invoked upon his enemy, goes home and--theoretically--lies down and dies. As a matter of fact, however, the shaman is always ready with other formulas by means of which he can ward off such fatal results, in consideration of a sufficient quantity of cloth.

Should the first trial, which takes place at daybreak, prove unsuccessful, the shaman and his client fast until just before sunset. They then eat and remain awake until midnight, when the ceremony is repeated, and if still unsuccessful it may be repeated four times before daybreak (or the following noon?), both men remaining awake and fasting throughout the night. If still unsuccessful, they continue to fast all day until just before sundown. Then they eat again and again remain awake until midnight, when the previous night's programme is repeated. It has now become a trial of endurance between the revengeful client and his shaman on the one side and the intended victim and his shaman on the other, the latter being supposed to be industriously working countercharms all the while, as each party must subsist upon one meal per day and abstain entirely from sleep until the result has been decided one way or the other. Failure to endure this severe strain, even so much as closing the eyes in sleep for a few moments or partaking of the least nourishment excepting just before sunset, neutralizes all the previous work and places the unfortunate offender at the mercy of his more watchful enemy. If the shaman be still unsuccessful on the fourth day, he acknowledges himself defeated and gives up the contest. Should his spells prove the stronger, his victim will die within seven days, or, as the Cherokees say, seven nights. These "seven nights," however, are frequently interpreted, figuratively, to mean seven years, a rendering which often serves to relieve the shaman from a very embarrassing position.

With regard to the oracle of the whole proceeding, the beads do move; but the explanation is simple, although the Indians account for it by saying that the beads become alive by the recitation of the sacred formula. The shaman is laboring under strong, though suppressed, emotion. He stands with his hands stretched out in a constrained position, every muscle tense, his breast heaving and voice trembling from the effort, and the natural result is that before he is done praying his fingers begin to twitch involuntarily and thus cause the beads to move. As before stated, their motion is irregular; but the peculiar delicacy of touch acquired by long practice probably imparts more directness to their movements than would at first seem possible.

THIS CONCERNS THE BALL PLAY--TO TAKE THEM TO WATER WITH IT

HIÄ' A`NE'TSÂ UGÛ'ⁿWA`LÏ AMÂ'YÏ DITSÛ'ⁿSTA`TÏ.

Sgë! Ha-nâgwa ä'stï une'ga aksâ'ûⁿtanû'ⁿ usïnu'lï a`ne'tsâ, unatsâ'nûⁿtse'lahï aktaˈˈtï adûⁿni'ga.

Iyu'stï utadâ'ta, iyu'stï tsunadâ'ita. Nûⁿnâ'hï anite'lahëhû' ige'skï nige'sûnna. Dû'ksi-gwû' dedu'natsgûˈla'wate'gû. Daˈˈsûⁿ unilâtsi'satû. Sa`ka'ni unati'satû'.

Nûⁿnâ'hï dâ'tadu'nina'watï' a'yû-`nû' digwatseli'ga a`ne'tsâ unatsâ'nûⁿtse'lahï. Tla'mehû Gigage'ï sâ'gwa danûtsgûˈˈlani'ga. Igü'ⁿyï galû'ⁿlâ ge'sûⁿ i'yûⁿ kanû'ⁿlagï ᵘwâhâ'hïstâ'gï. Ta'line galû'ⁿlâ ge'sûⁿ i'yûⁿ kanû'ⁿlagï ᵘwâhâ'hïstâ'gï. He'nilû danûtsgûˈˈlani'ga. Tla'ma ûⁿni'ta a'nigwalu'gi gûⁿtlaˈˈtisge'stï, ase'gwû nige'sûⁿna.

Du'talë a`ne'tsâ unatsâ'nûntse'lahï saligu'gi-gwû dedu'natsgûˈˈlawïsti'tegû'. Elawi'nï daˈˈsûⁿ unilâtsi'satû.

Tsâ'ine digalû'ⁿlatiyû'ⁿ Sâ'niwä Gi'gageï sâ'gwa danûtsgûˈˈlani'ga, asë`gâ'gï nige'sûⁿna. Kanû'ⁿlagï ᵘwâhâ'hïstâ'gï nûˈˈgine digalû'ⁿlatiyû'ⁿ. Gulïˈsgulï' Sa`ka'ni sâ'gwa danûtsgûˈˈlani'ga, asë`gâ'gïnig'esuⁿna. Kanû'ⁿlagï ᵘwâhâ'hïstâgï hï'skine digalû'ⁿlatiyû'ⁿ. Tsütsü' Sa`ka'ni sâ'gwa danûtsgûˈˈlani'ga, asë`gâ'gï nige'sûⁿna.

Du'talë a`ne'tsâ utsâ'nûⁿtse'lahï. Tïne'gwa Sa`ka'ni sâ'gwa danûtsgûˈˈlani'ga, ige'skï nige'sûⁿna. Daˈˈsûⁿ unilâtsi'satû. Kanû'ⁿlagï ᵘwâhâ'hïstâ'gï sutali'ne digalû'ⁿlatiyû'ⁿ. A'nigâsta'ya sâ'gwa danûtsgûˈˈlani'ga, asë`gâ'gï nige'sûⁿna. Kanû'ⁿlagï ᵘwâhâ'hïstâ'gï kûl`kwâgine digalû'ⁿlatiyû'ⁿ. Wâtatû'ga Sa`ka'ni sâ'gwa danûtsgûˈˈlani'ga, asë`gâ'gï nige'sûⁿna.

Du'talë a`ne'tsâ unatsâ'nûⁿtse'lahï, Yâ'na dedu'natsgûˈˈlawïstani'ga, ige'skï nige'suⁿna. Da`sûⁿ du'nilâtsi'satû. Kanû'ⁿlagï de'tagaskalâ'ûⁿtanû'ⁿ, igûⁿ'wûlstanûhi-gwûdi'na tsuye'listi gesû'ⁿï. Akta'ᵗï adûⁿni'ga.

Sgë! Nâ'gwa t?skï'nâne'lï ta'tädü' iyû'ⁿta a'gwatseli'ga, Wätatu'ga Tsûne'ga. Tsuye'listï gesû'ⁿï skï'nâhûⁿsï' a'gwatseli'ga--kanû'ⁿlagï a'gwatseli'ga. Nä'ᵗnâ utadâ'ta kanû'ⁿlagï dedu'skalâ'asi'ga.

Dedû'ndagû'ⁿyastani'ga, gûⁿwâ'hisâ'nûhï. Yû!

Translation.

THIS CONCERNS THE BALL PLAY--TO TAKE THEM TO WATER WITH IT.

Listen! Ha! Now where the white thread has been let down, quickly we are about to examine into (the fate of) the admirers of the ball play.

They are of--such a (iyu'stï) descent. They are called--so and so (iyu'stï). They are shaking the road which shall never be joyful. The miserable Terrapin has come and fastened himself upon them as they go about. They have lost all strength. They have become entirely blue.

But now my admirers of the ball play have their roads lying along in this direction. The Red Bat has come and made himself one of them. There in the first heaven are the pleasing stakes. Therein the second heaven are the pleasing stakes. The Pewee has come and joined them. The immortal ball stick shall place itself upon the whoop, never to be defeated.

As for the lovers of the ball play on the other side, the common Turtle has come and fastened himself upon them as they go about. Under the earth they have lost all strength.

The pleasing stakes are in the third heaven. The Red Tläniwä has come and made himself one of them, that they may never be defeated. The pleasing stakes are in the fourth heaven. The Blue Fly-catcher has made himself one of them, that they may never be defeated. The pleasing stakes are in the fifth heaven. The Blue Martin has made himself one of them, that they may never be defeated.

The other lovers of the ball play, the Blue Mole has come and fastened upon them, that they may never be joyous. They have lost all strength.

The pleasing stakes are there in the sixth heaven. The Chimney Swift has made himself one of them, that they may never be defeated. The pleasing stakes are in the seventh heaven. The Blue Dragon-fly has made himself one of them, that they may never be defeated.

As for the other admirers of the ball play, the Bear has just come and fastened him upon them, that they may never be happy. They have lost all strength. He has let the stakes slip from his grasp and there shall be nothing left for their share.

The examination is ended.

Listen! Now let me know that the twelve are mine, O White Dragon-fly. Tell me that the share is to be mine--that the stakes are mine. As for the player there on the other side, he has been forced to let go his hold upon the stakes.

Now they are become exultant and happy. Yû

Explanation.

This formula, from the A`yûninï manuscript is one of those used by the shaman in taking the ball players to water before the game. The ceremony is performed in connection with red and black beads, as described in the formula just given for destroying life. The formulistic name given to the ball players signifies literally, "admirers of the ball play." The Tlä'niwä (sä'niwä, in the Middle dialect) is the mythic great hawk, as large and powerful as the roc of Arabian tales. The shaman begins by declaring that it is his purpose to examine or inquire into the fate of the ball players, and then gives his attention by turns to his friends and their opponents, fixing his eyes upon the red bead while praying for his clients, and upon the black bead while speaking of their rivals. His friends he raises gradually to the seventh or highest *galû'^{n}lati*. This word literally signifies height, and is the name given to the abode of the gods dwelling above the earth, and is also used to mean heaven in the Cherokee bible translation. The opposing players, on the other hand, are put down under the earth, and are made to resemble animals slow and clumsy of movement, while on behalf of his friends the shaman invokes the aid of swift-flying birds, which, according to the Indian belief, never by any chance fail to secure their prey. The birds invoked are the He'nilû or wood pewee (*Contopus virens*), the Tläniwä or mythic hawk, the Gulï'sgulï' or great crested flycatcher (*Myiarchus crinitus*), the Tsûtsû or martin (*Progne subis*), and the A'nigâsta'ya or chimney swift (*Chœtura pelasgia*). In the idiom of the formulas it is said that these "have just come and are sticking to them" (the players), the same word (*danûtsgû'lani?ga*) being used to express the devoted attention of a lover to his mistress. The Watatuga, a small species of dragon-fly, is also invoked, together with the bat, which, according to a Cherokee myth, once took sides with the birds in a great ball contest with the four-footed animals, and won the victory for the birds by reason of his superior skill in dodging. This myth explains also why birds, and no quadrupeds, are invoked by the shaman to the aid of his friends. In accordance with the regular color symbolism the flycatcher, martin, and dragonfly, like the bat and the tlä'niwä, should be red, the color of success, instead of blue, evidently so written by mistake. The white thread is frequently mentioned in the formulas, but in this instance the reference is not clear. The twelve refers to the number of runs made in the game.

Made in United States
Troutdale, OR
11/21/2024